COLORFUL COUNTRYSIDE

COLORING BOOK

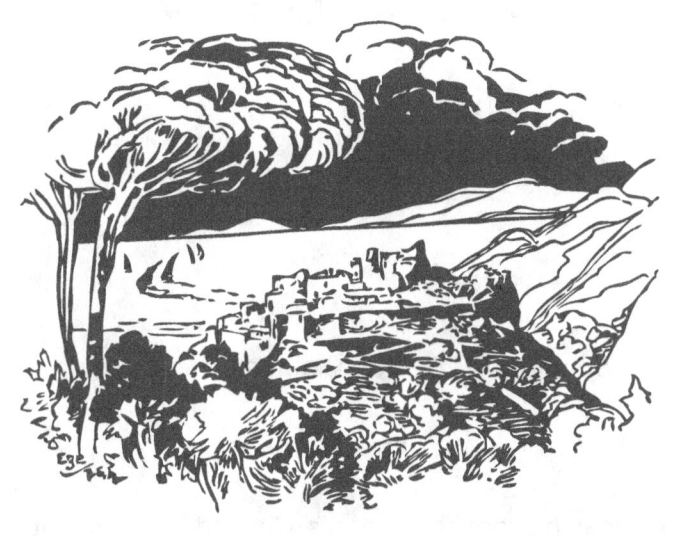

THANK YOU FOR CHOOSING OUR "COLORFUL COUNTRYSIDE" BOOK TO BE A PART OF YOUR CREATIVE JOURNEY. WE APPRECIATE YOUR TRUST IN OUR ABILITY TO PROVIDE YOU WITH A BEAUTIFUL AND RELAXING COLORING EXPERIENCE. WE HAVE WORKED HARD TO CURATE A COLLECTION OF INTRICATE AND SERENE DESIGNS THAT WILL TRANSPORT YOU TO THE IDYLLIC COUNTRYSIDE, AWAY FROM THE HUSTLE AND BUSTLE OF DAILY LIFE. WE HOPE THAT THIS BOOK WILL BRING YOU PEACE, TRANQUILITY, AND A SENSE OF JOY AS YOU BRING THESE ILLUSTRATIONS TO LIFE WITH YOUR FAVORITE COLORS. ONCE AGAIN, THANK YOU FOR YOUR SUPPORT AND WE HOPE YOU ENJOY YOUR COLORING JOURNEY WITH US.

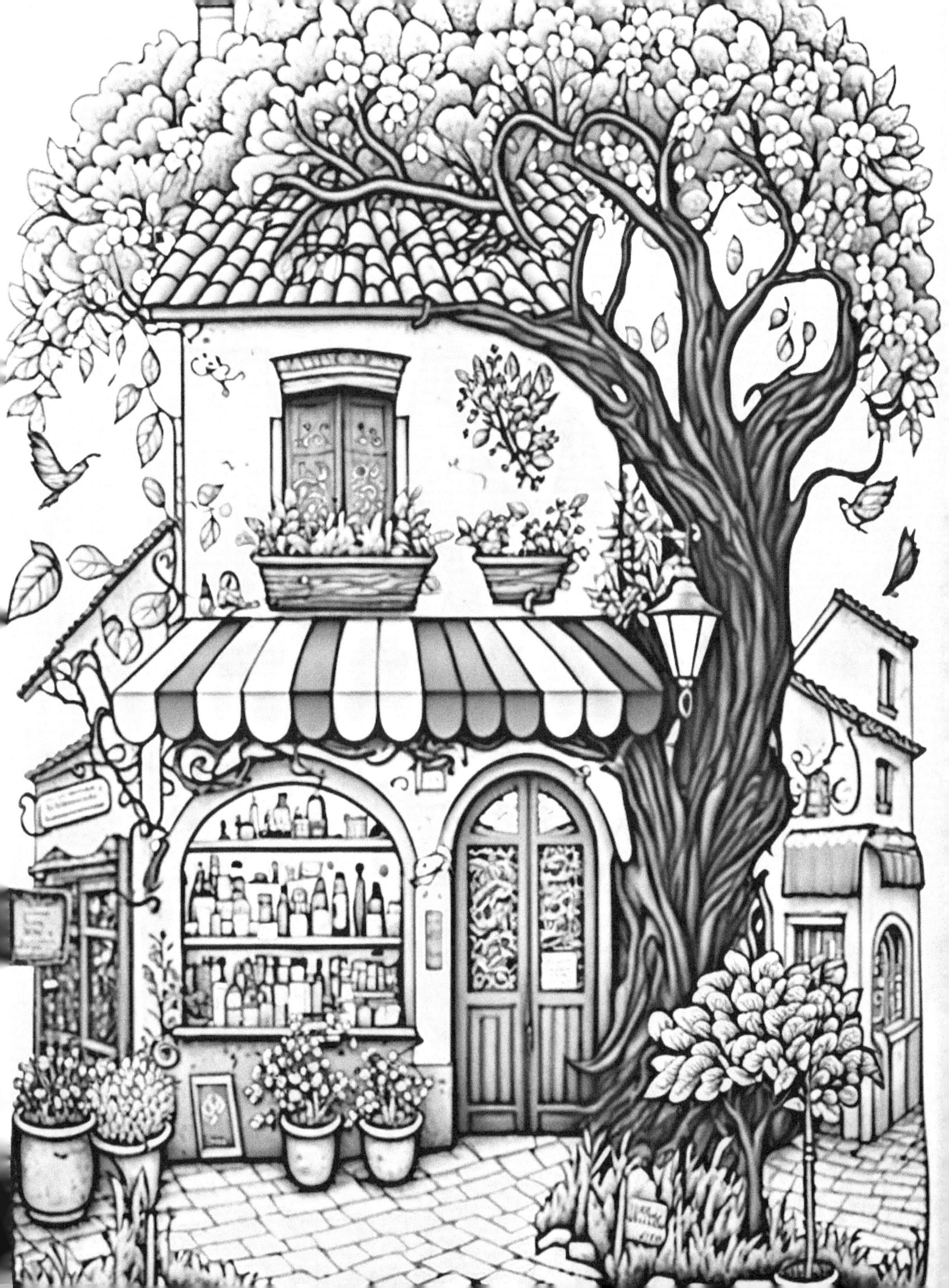

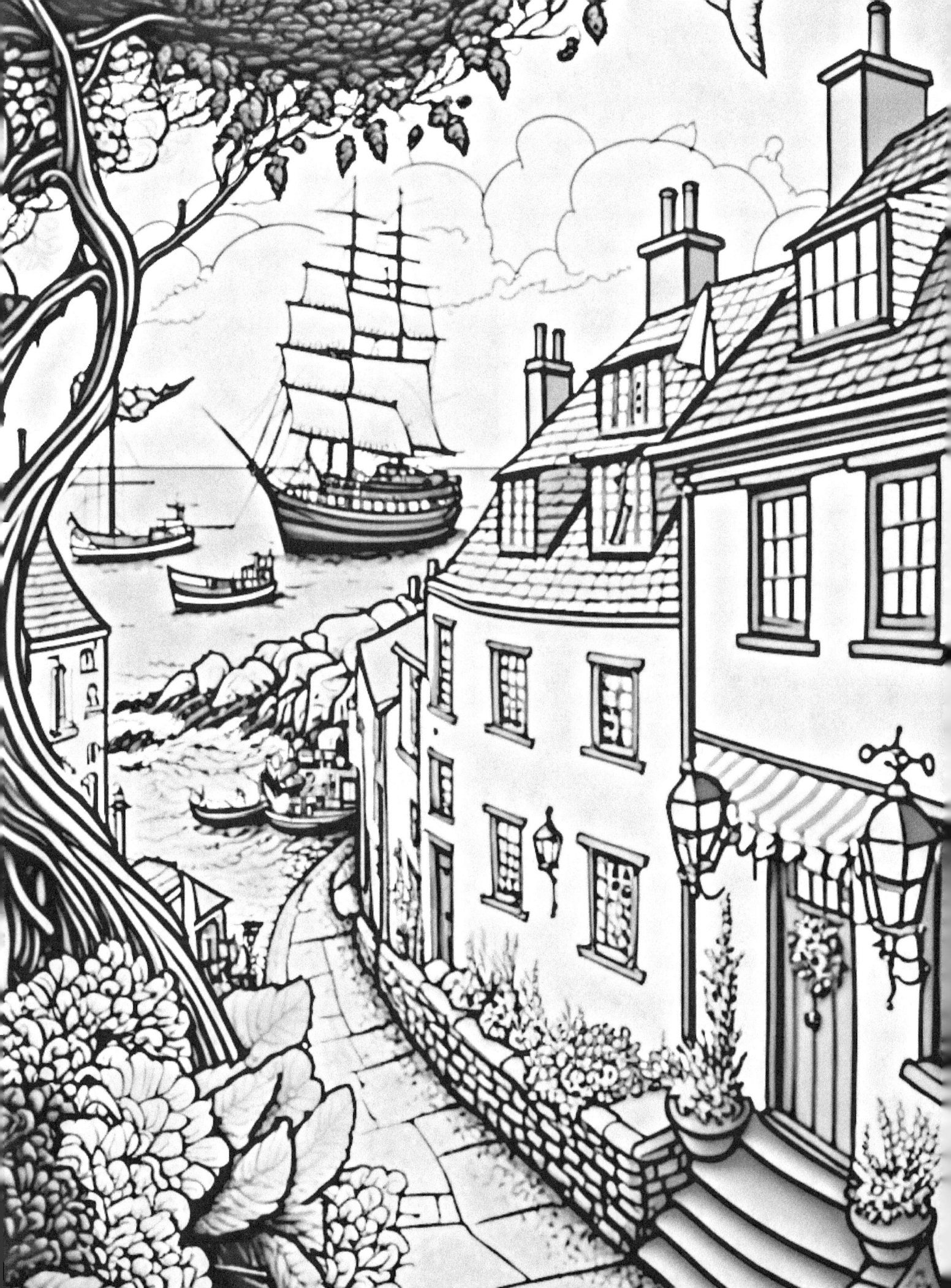

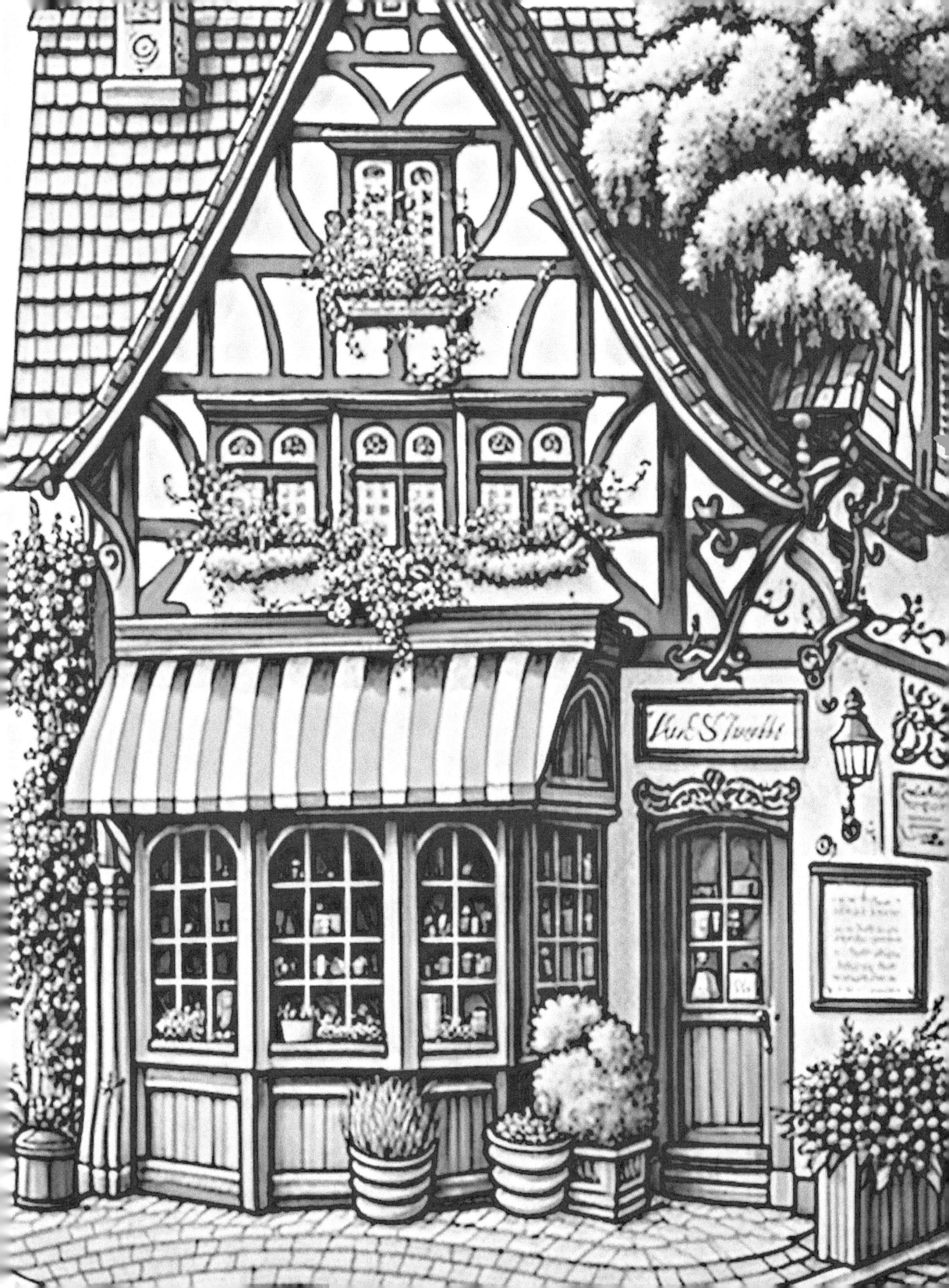

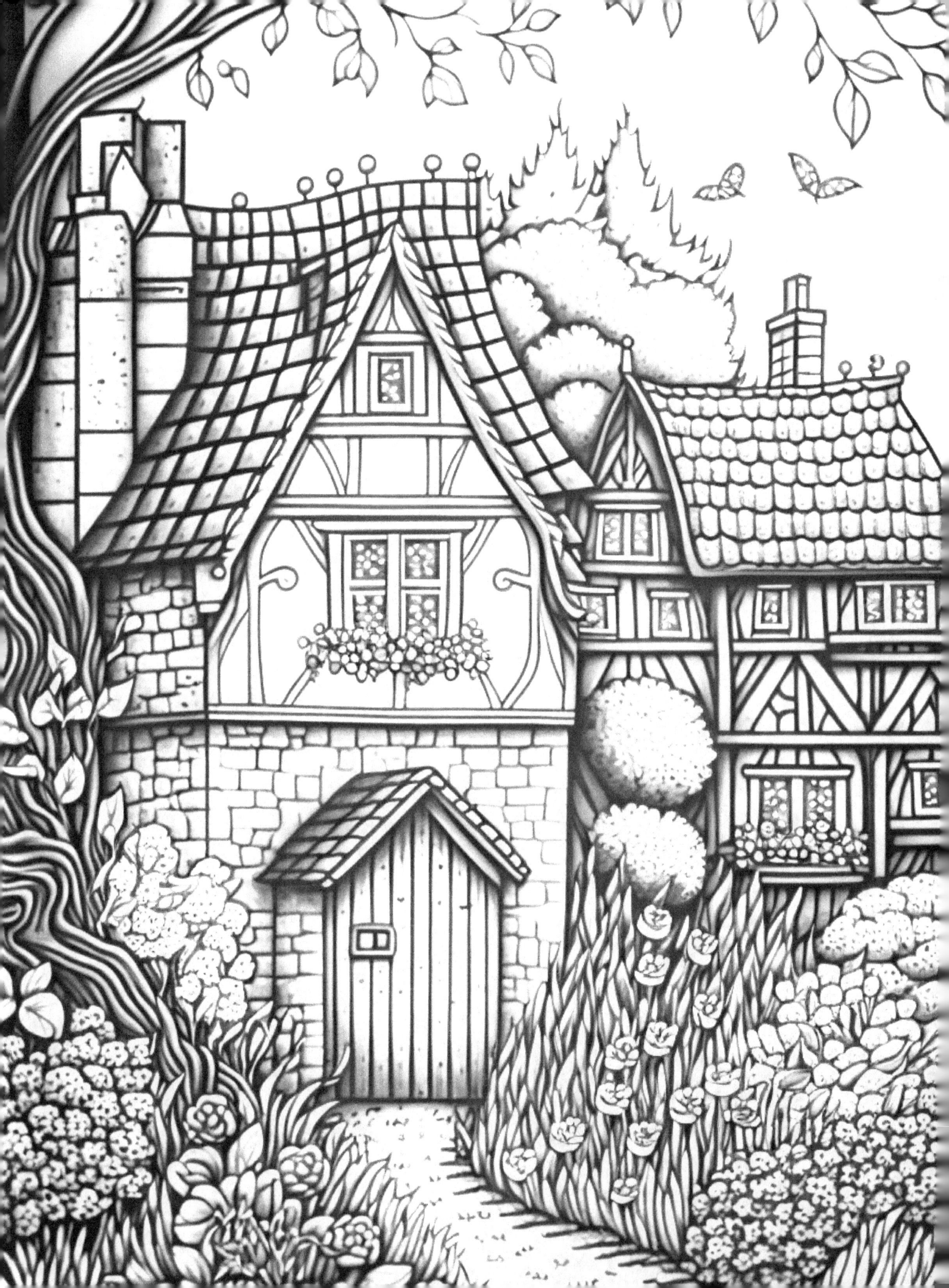

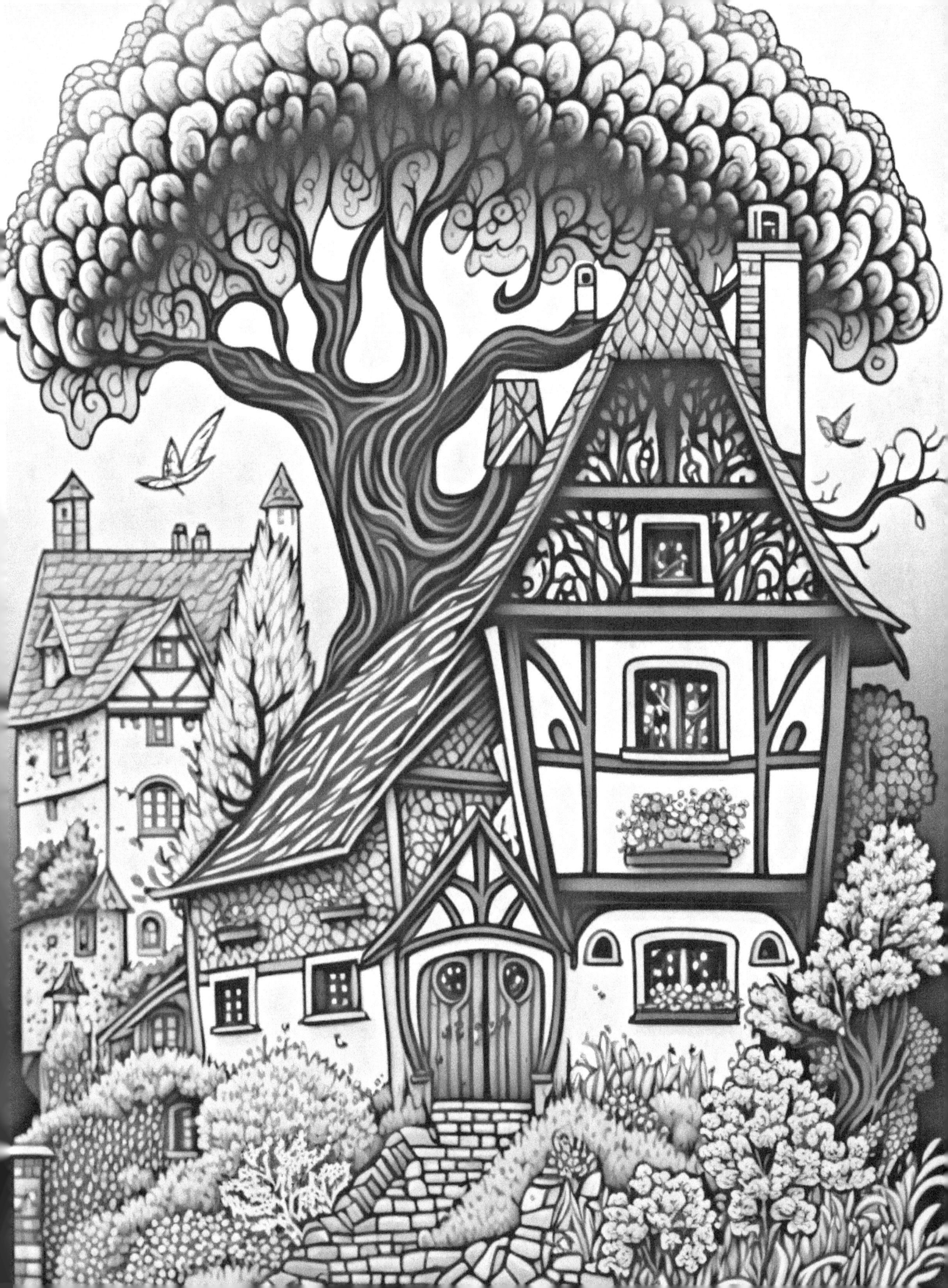

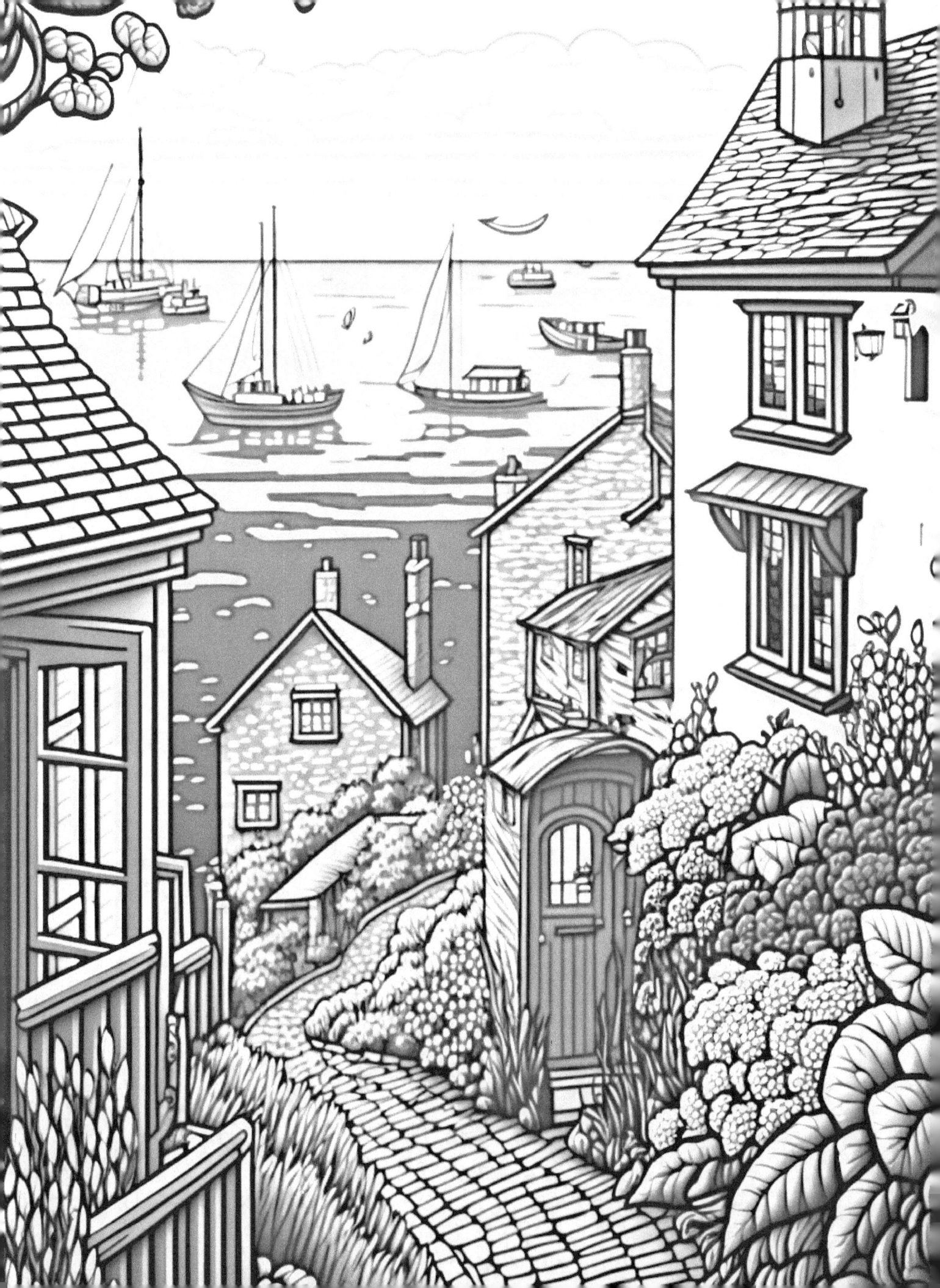

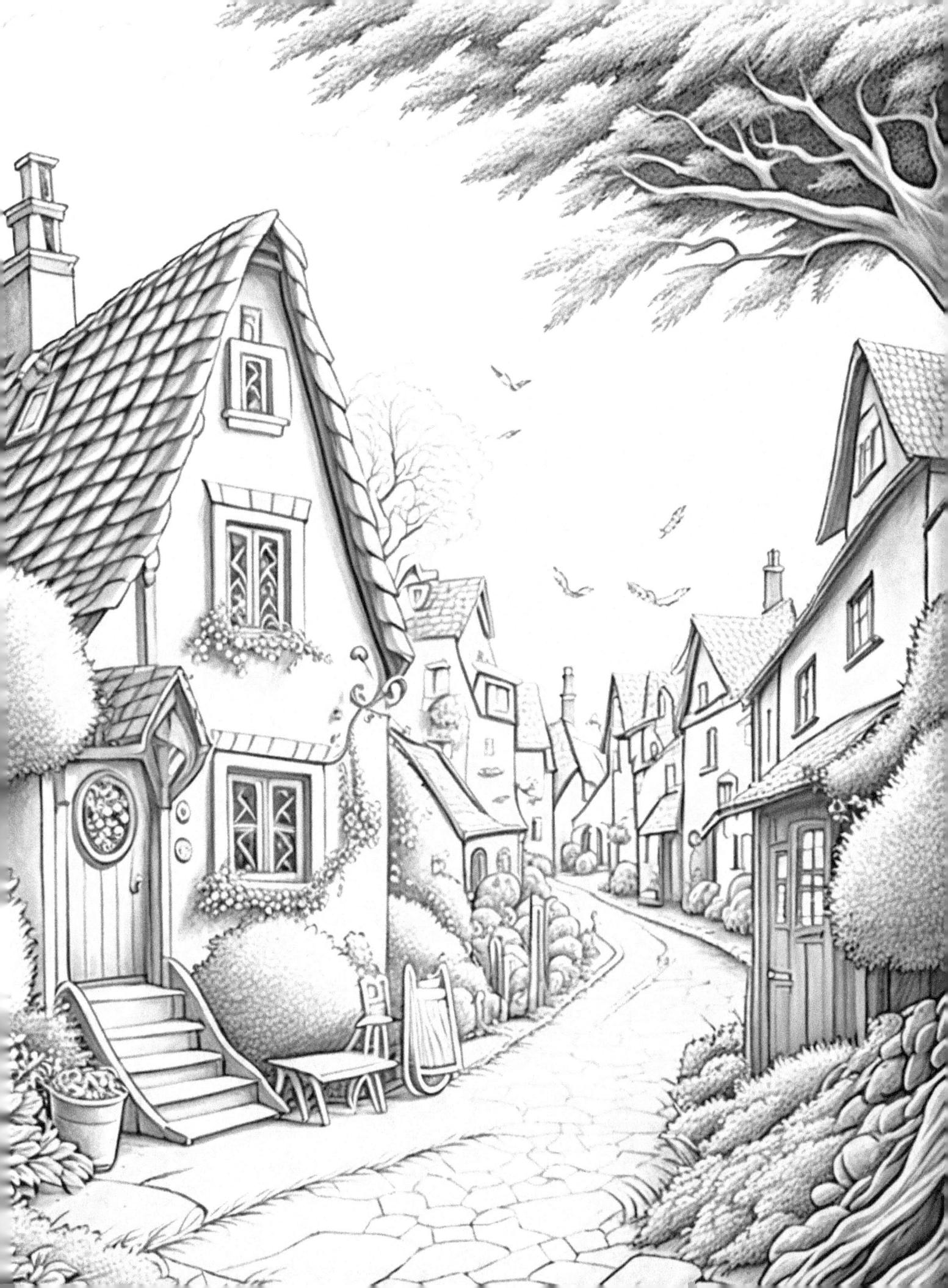

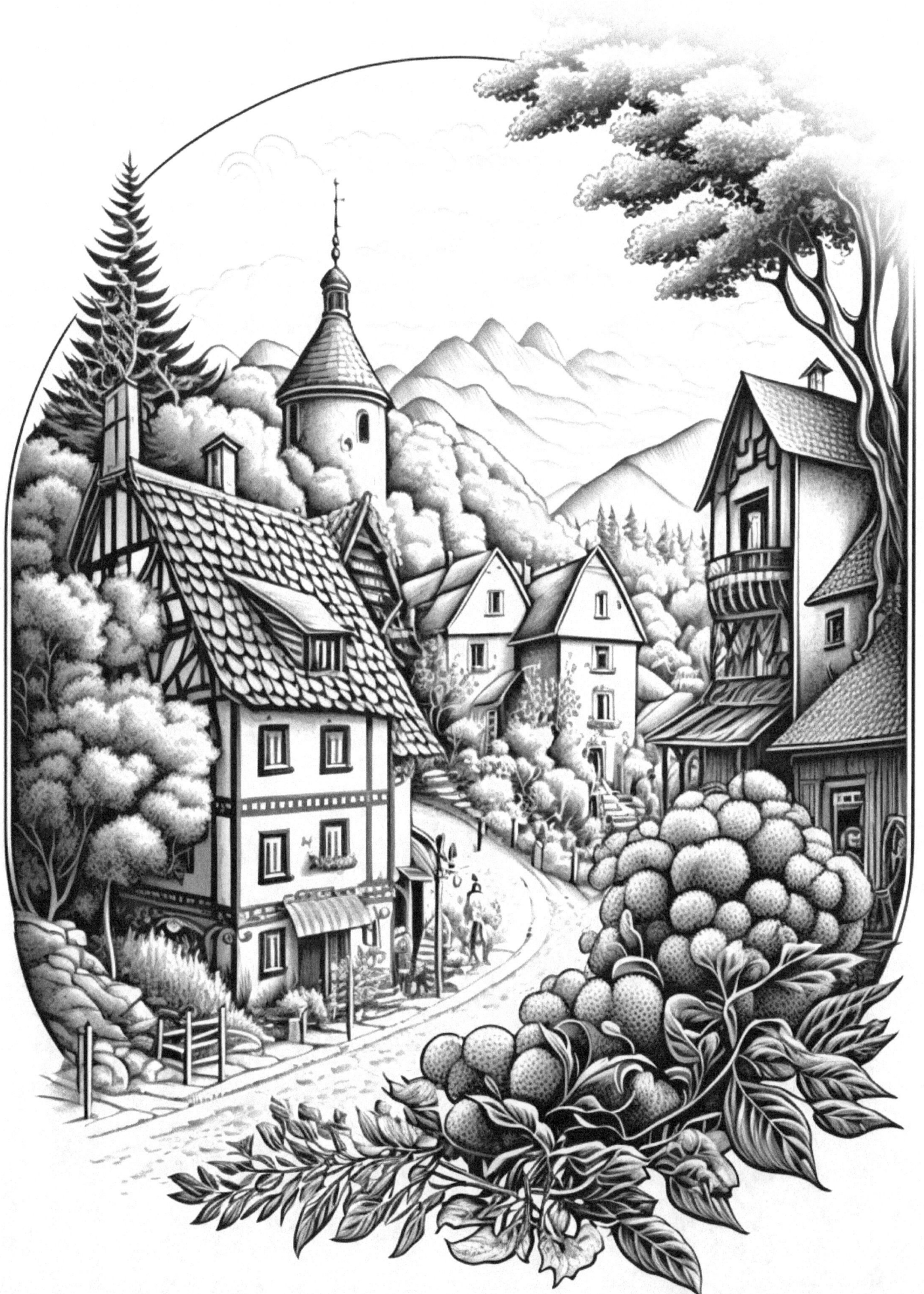

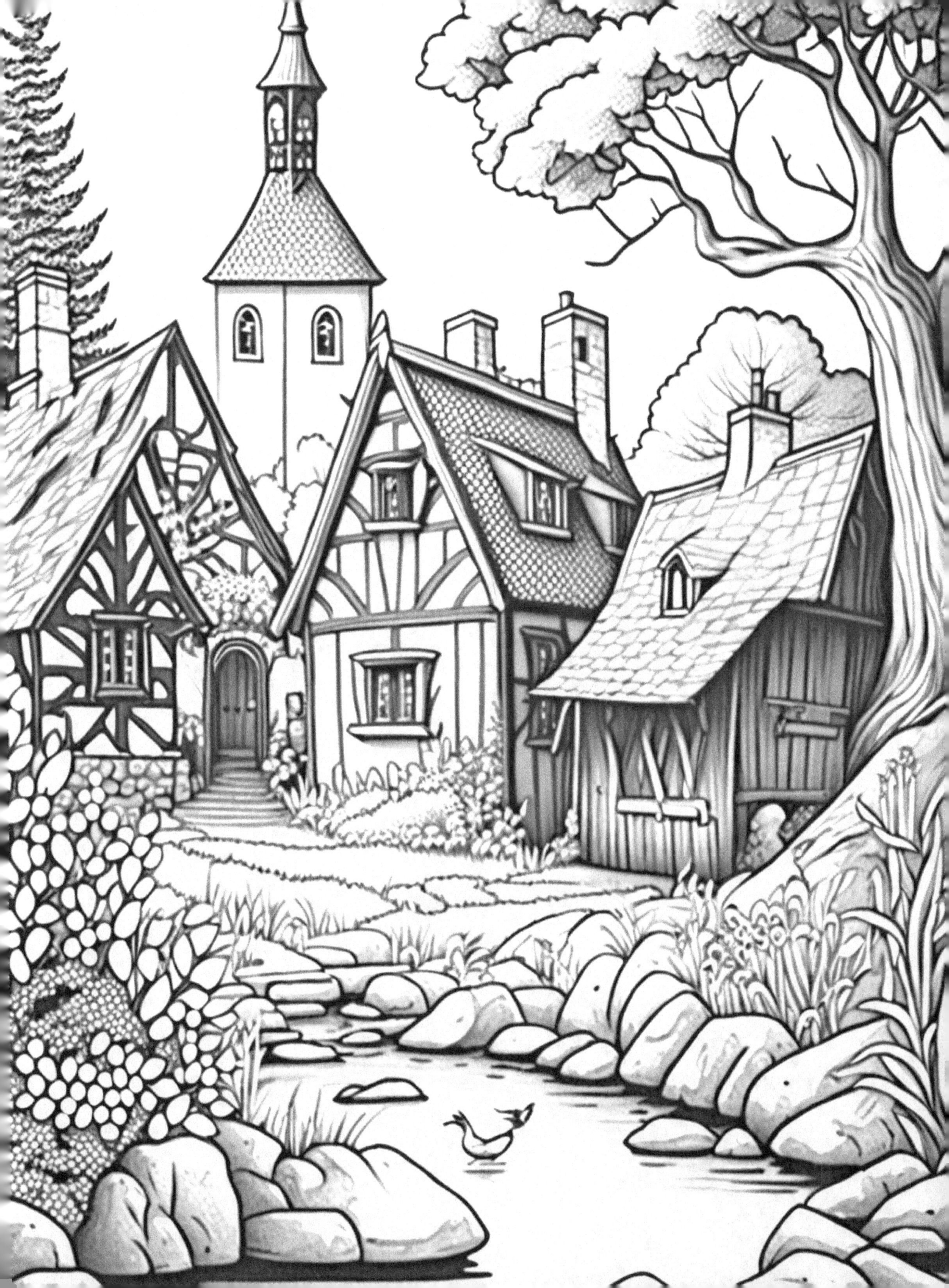

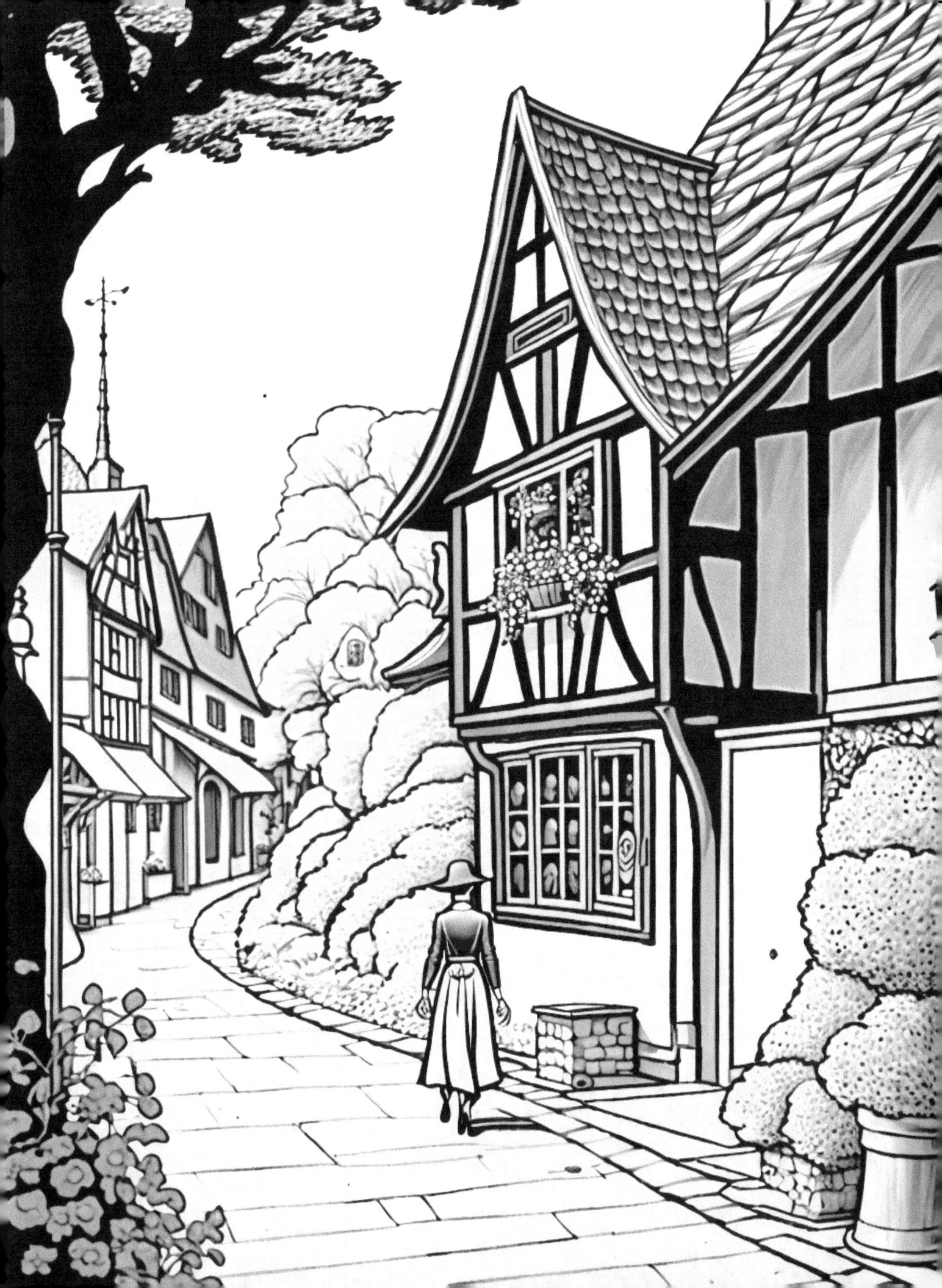

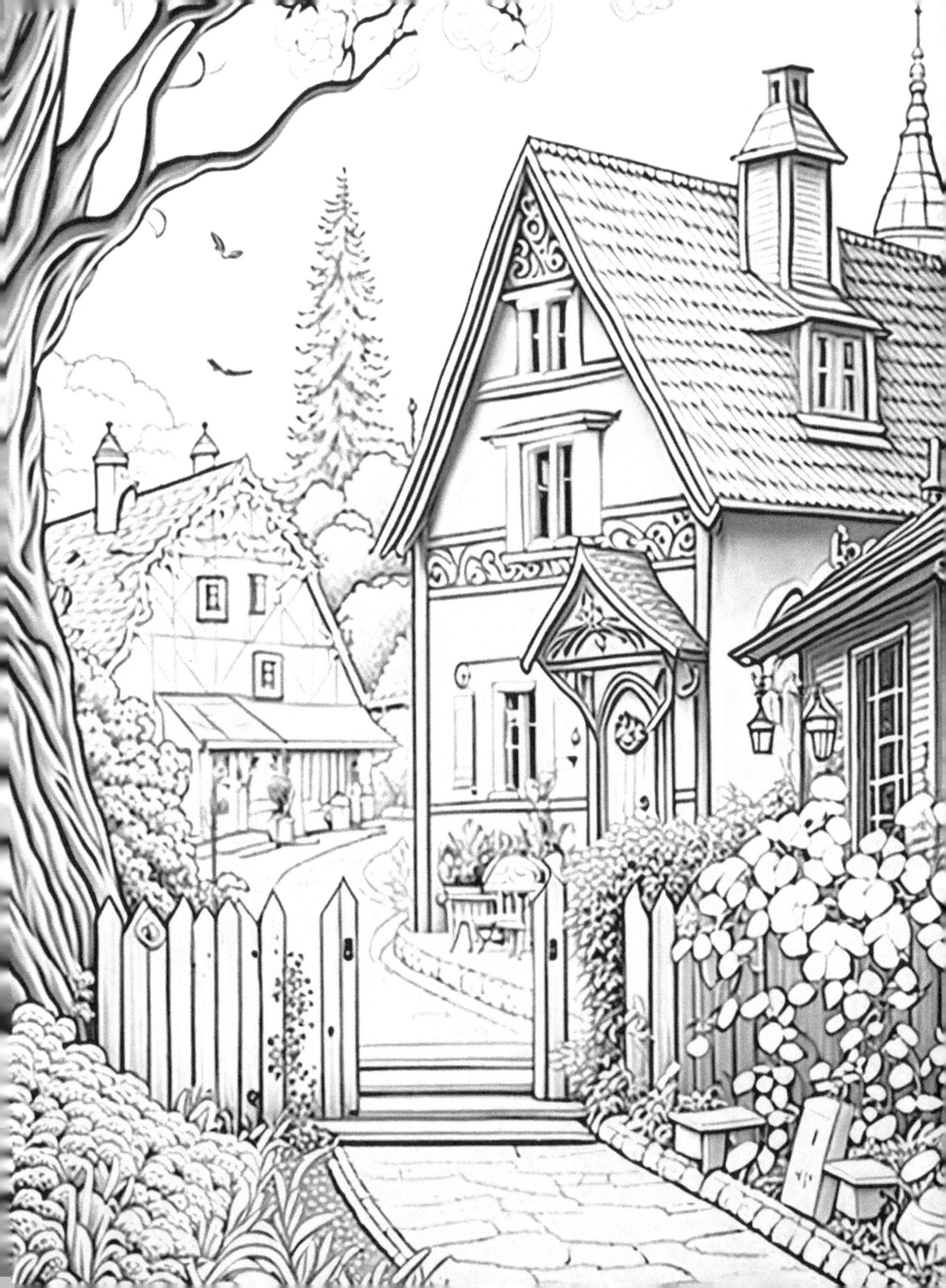

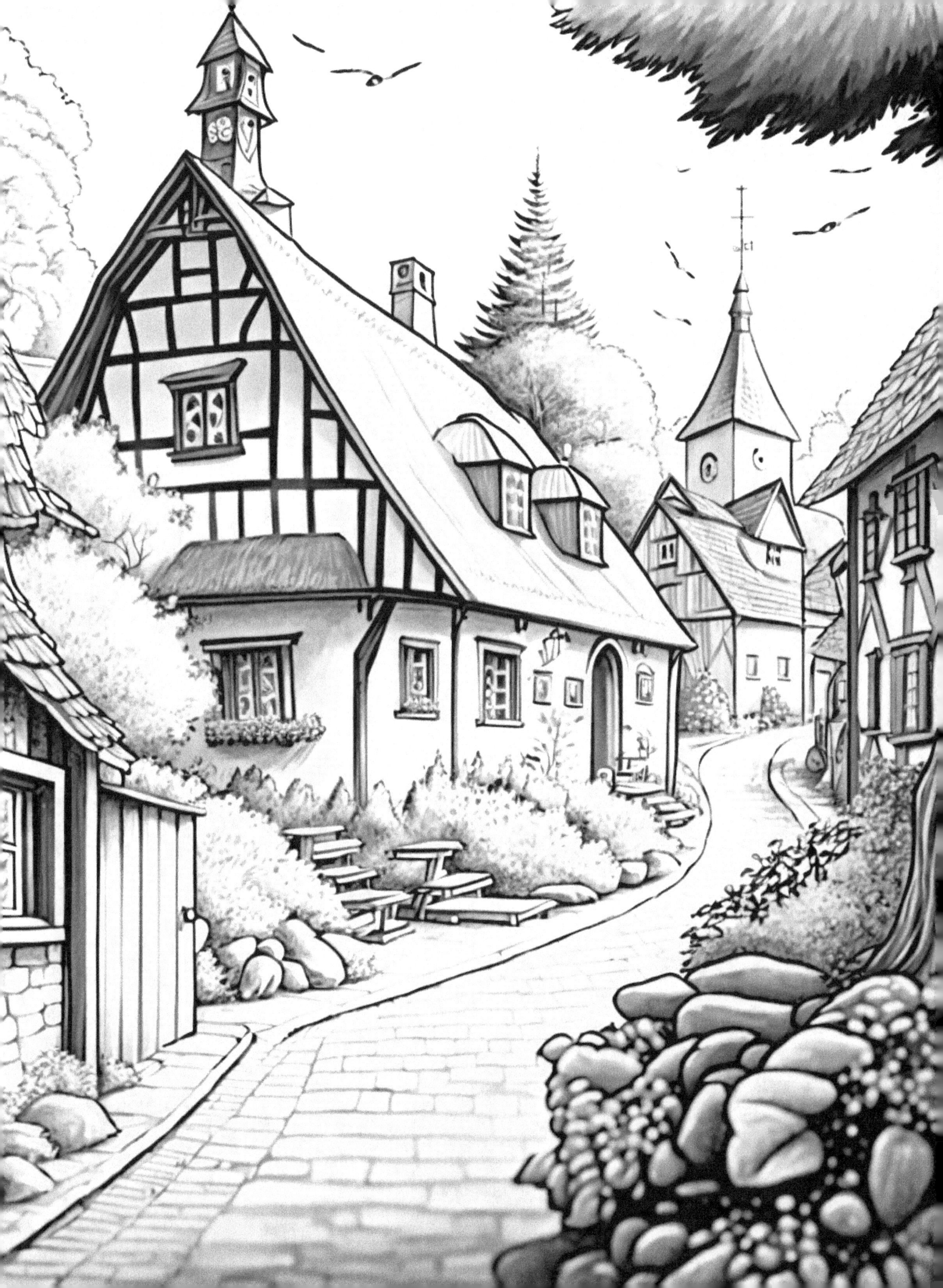

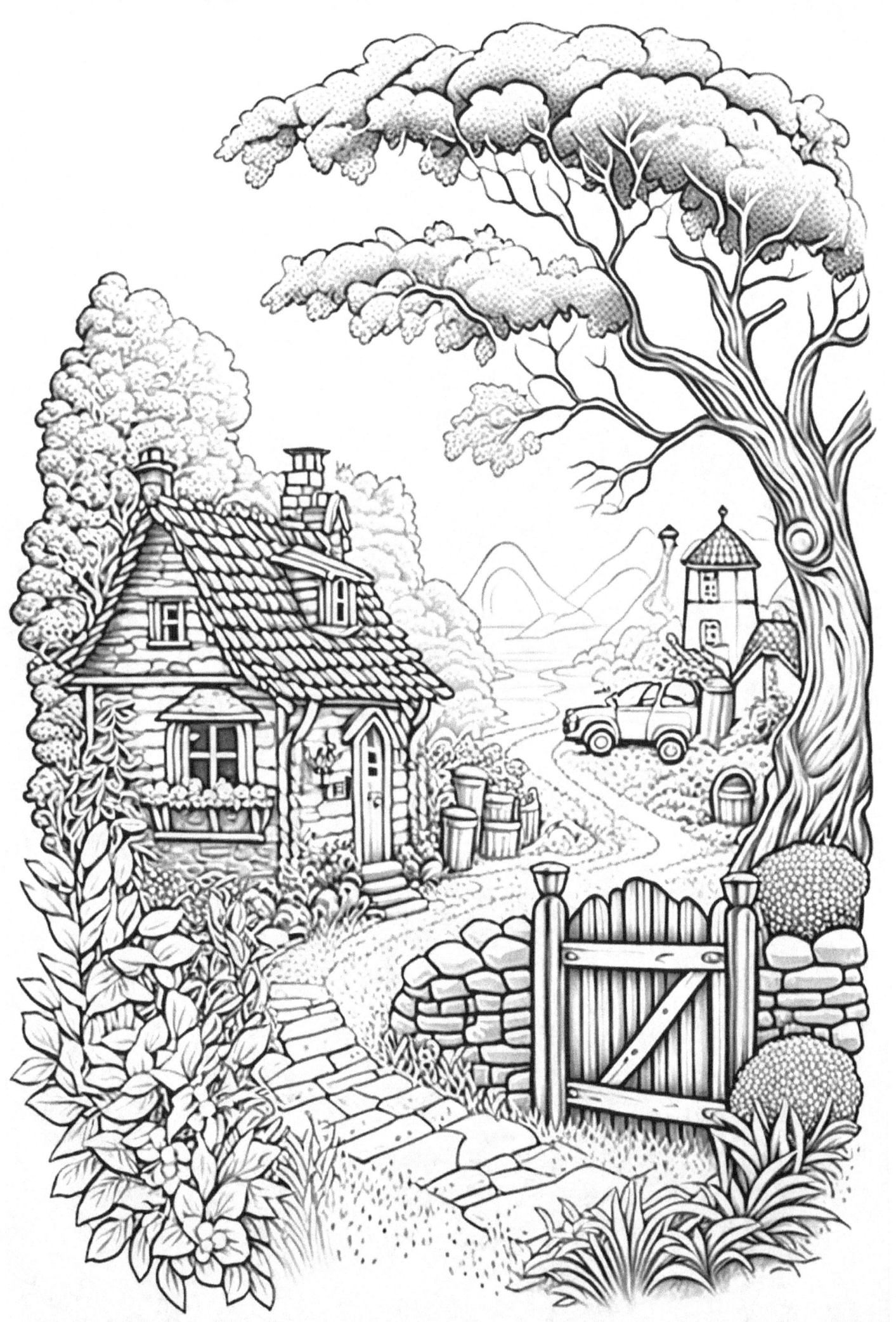

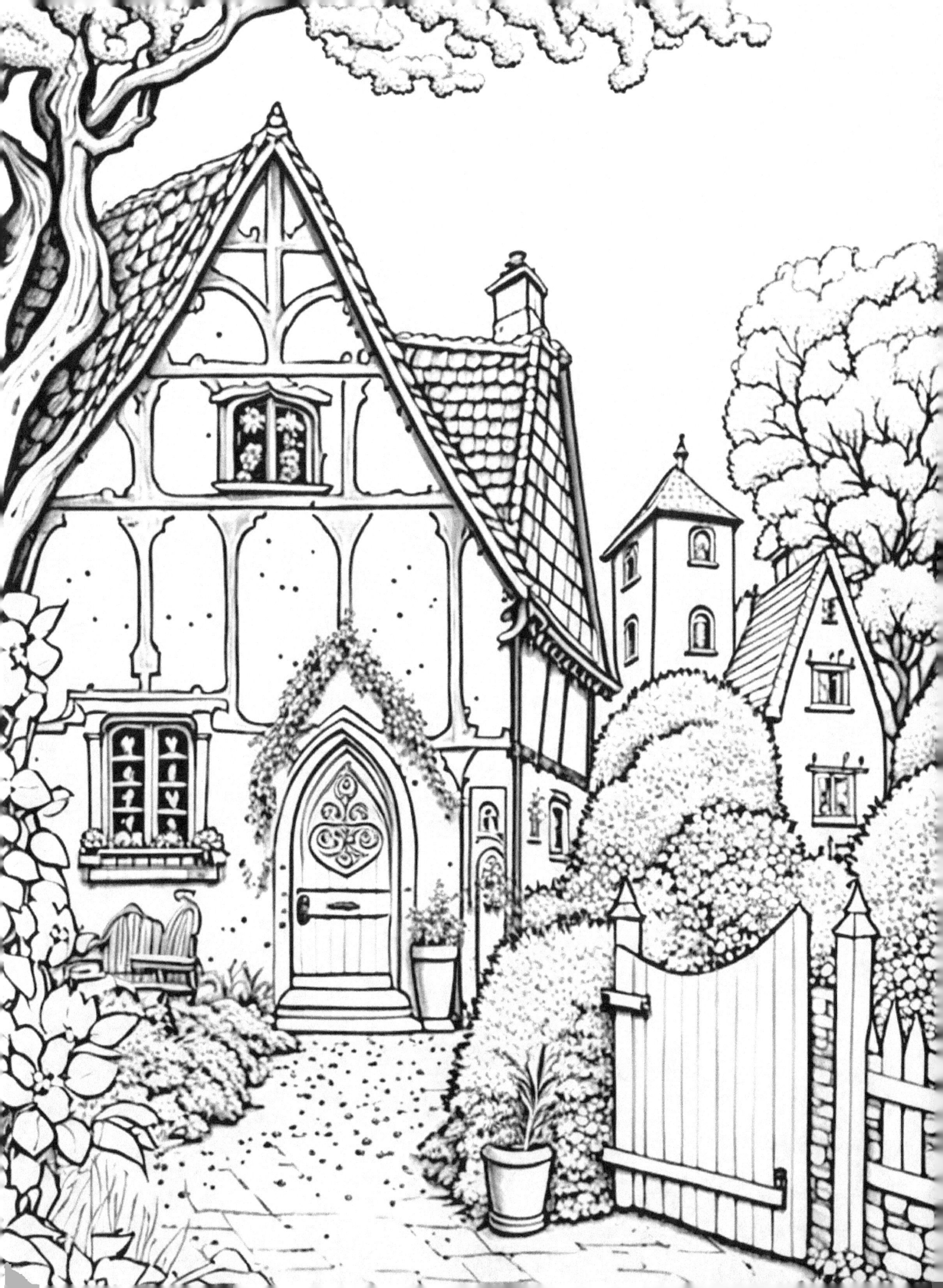

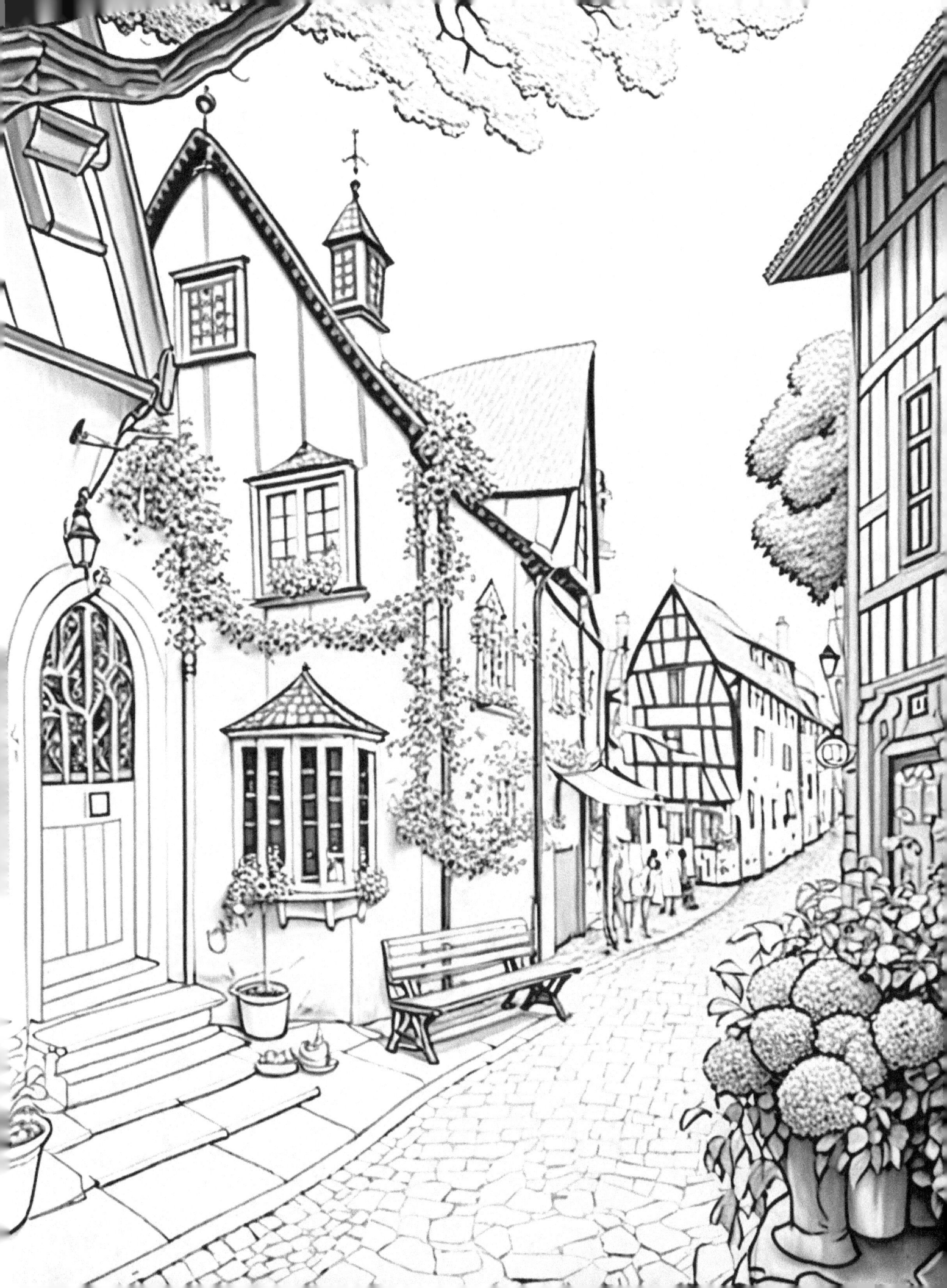

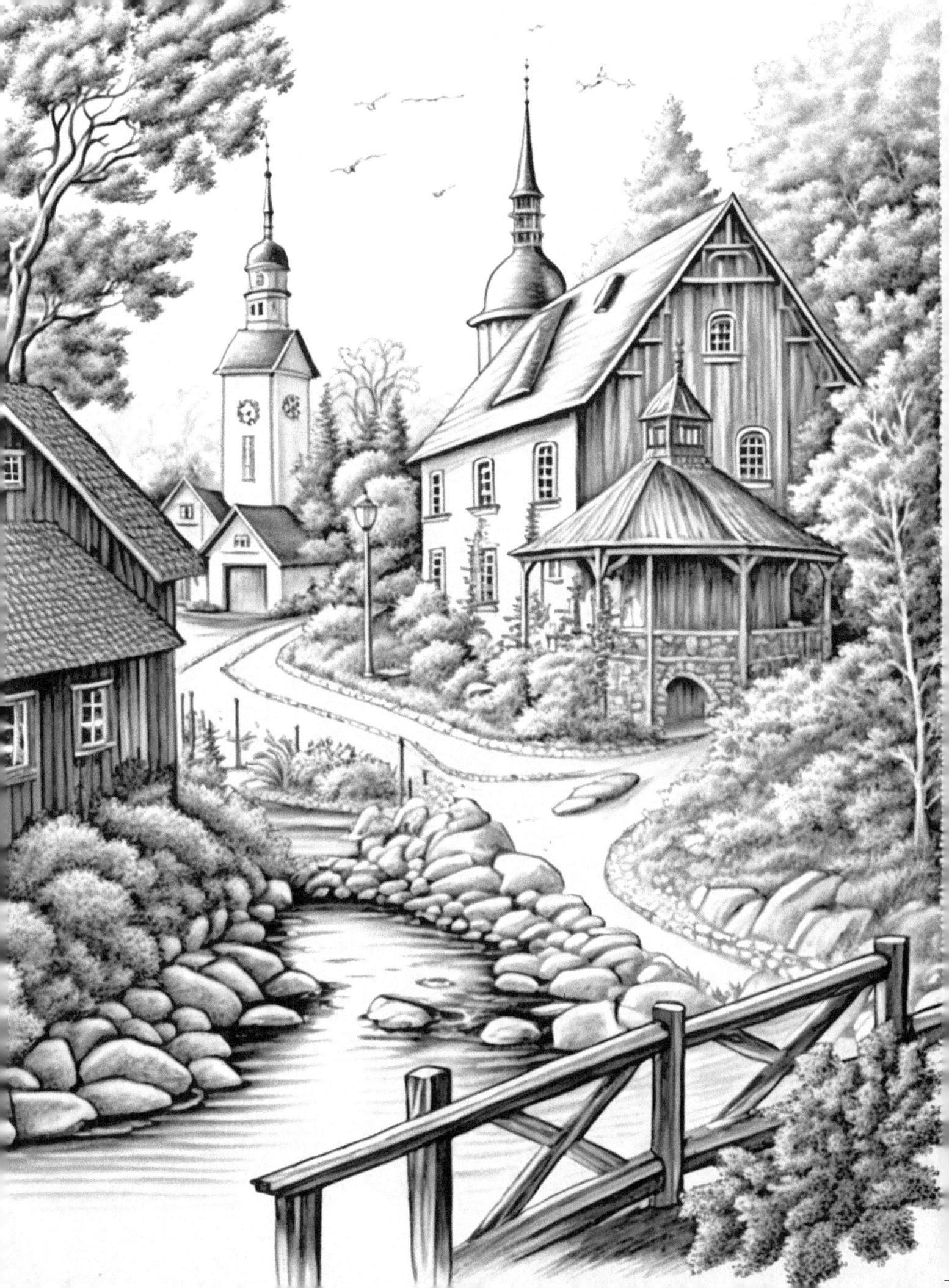

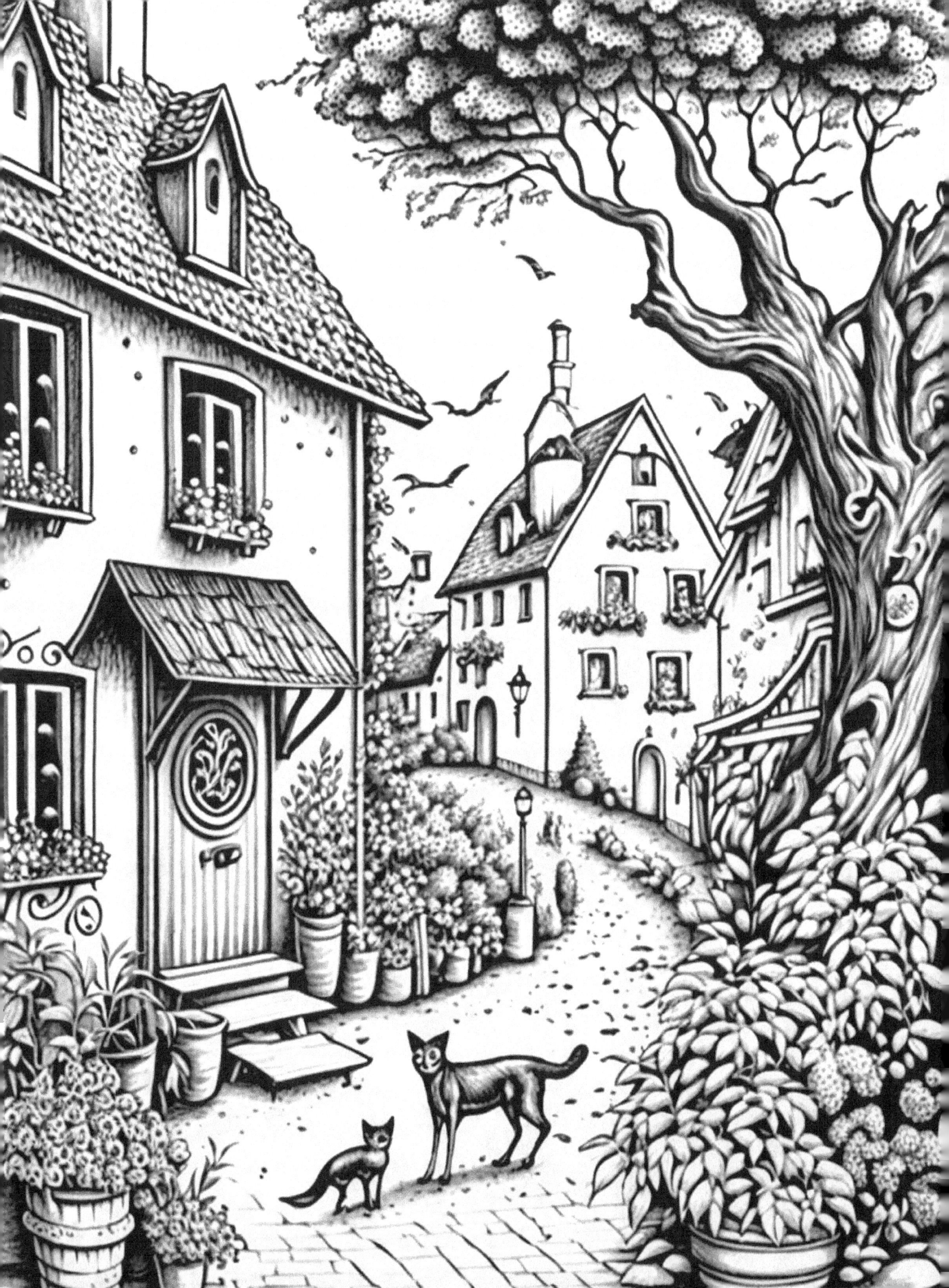

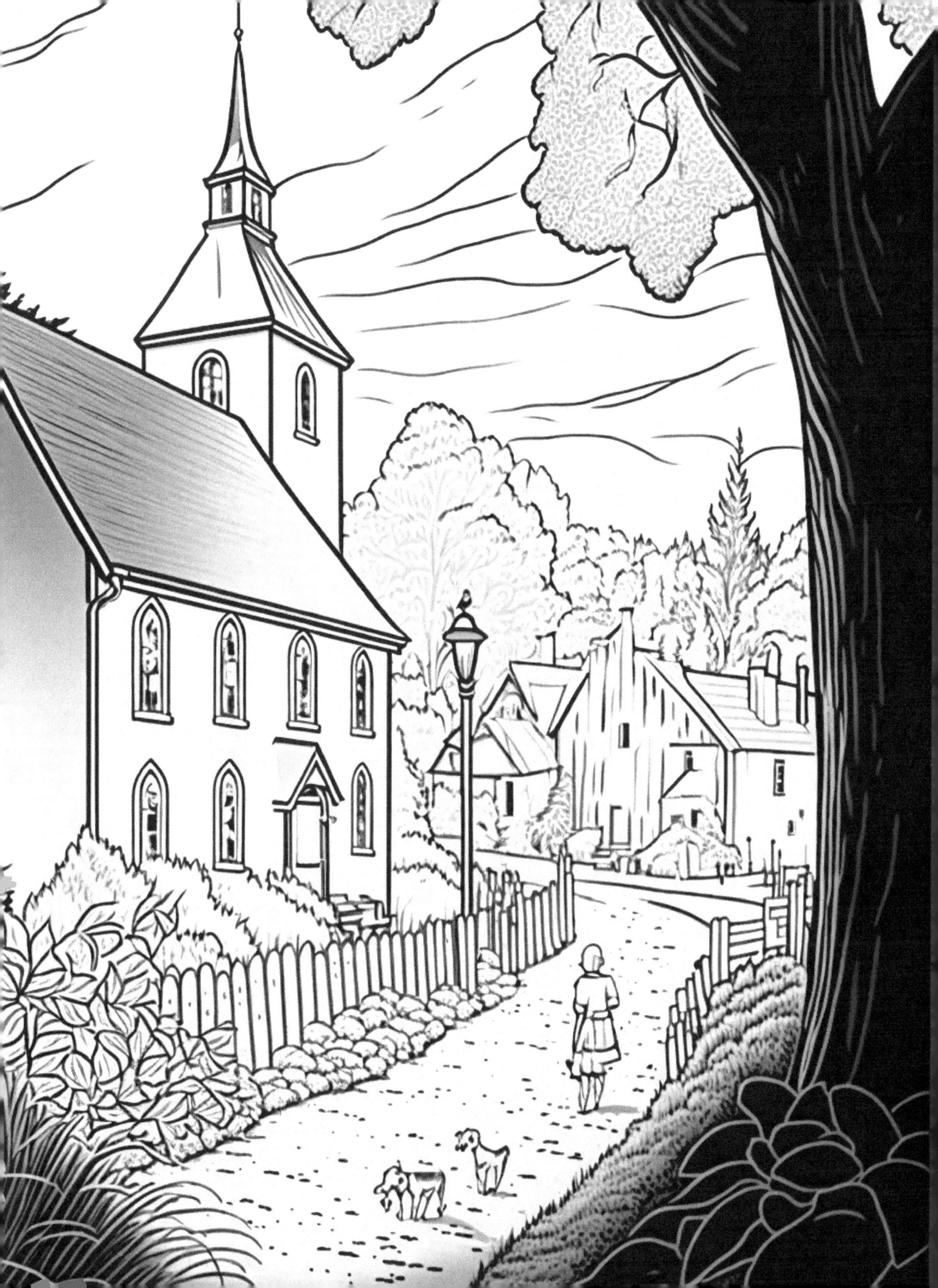

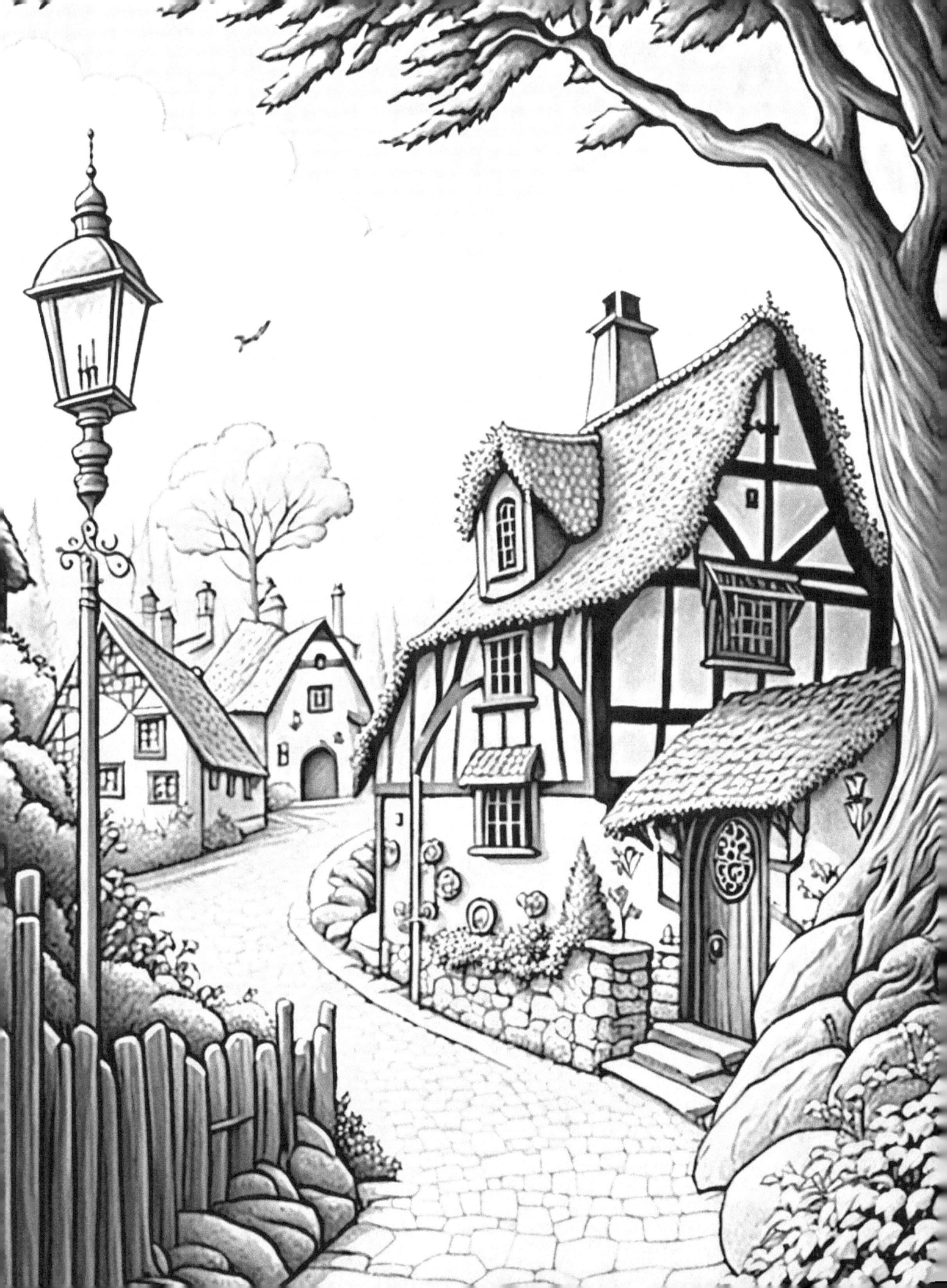

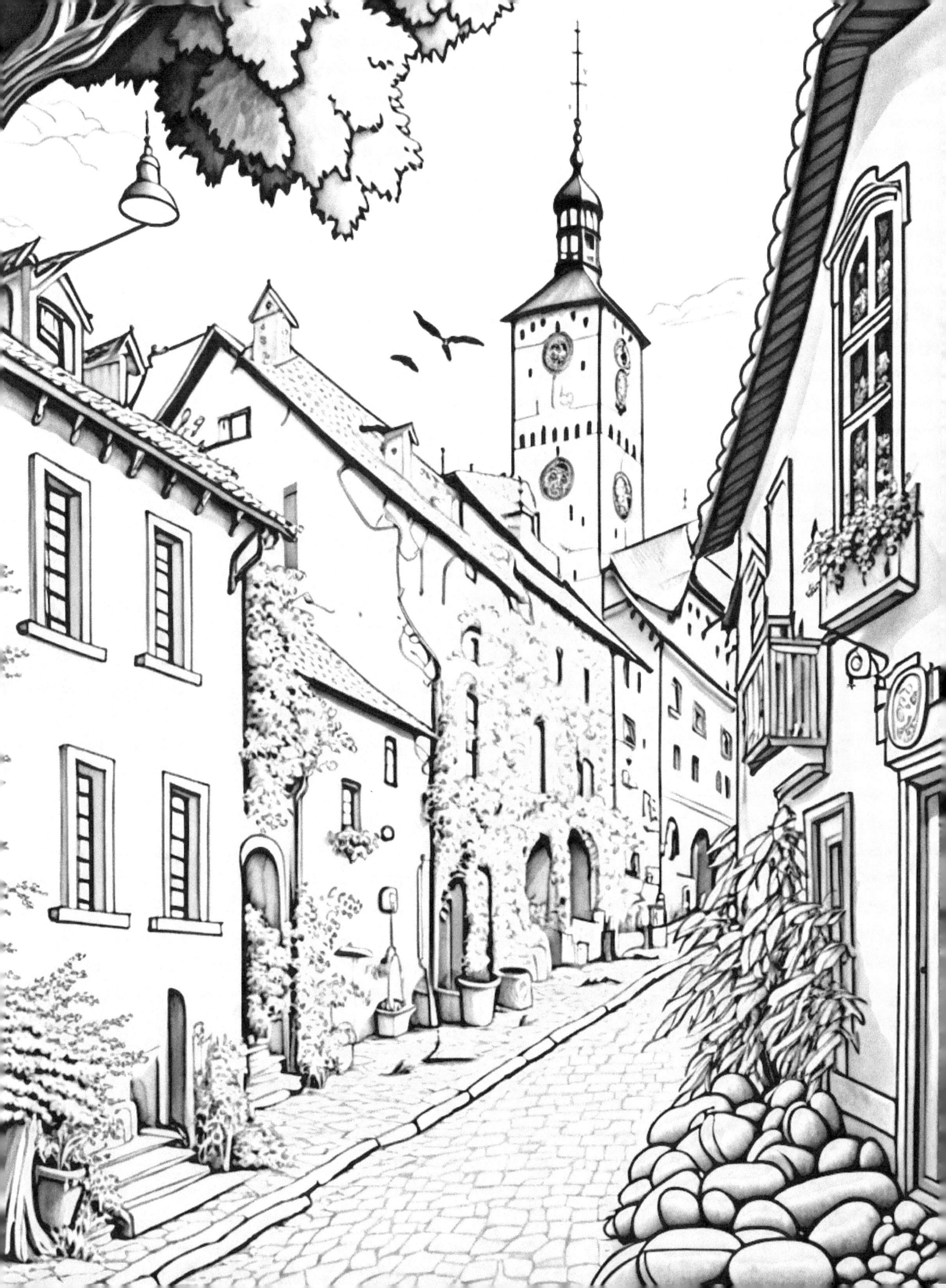

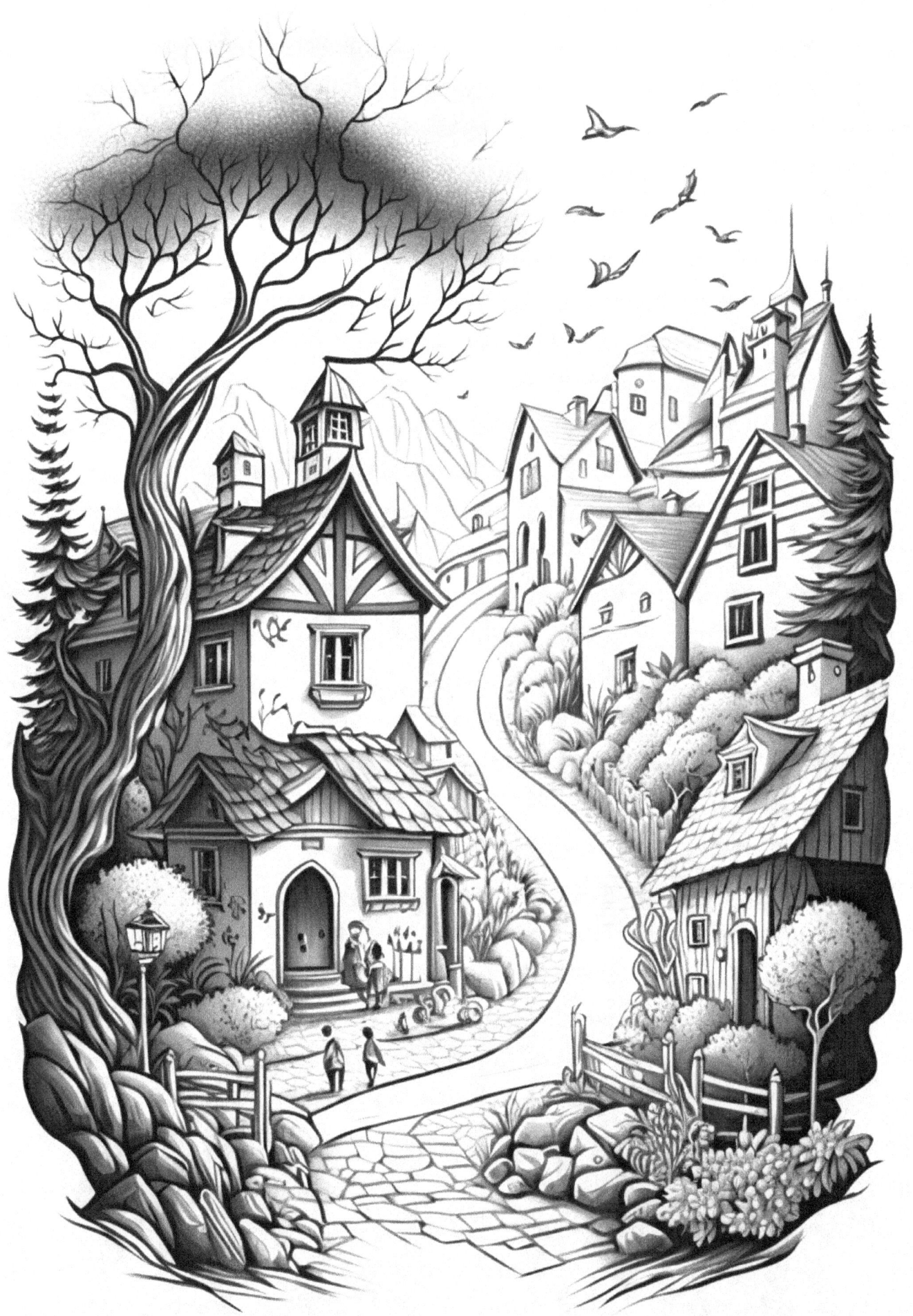

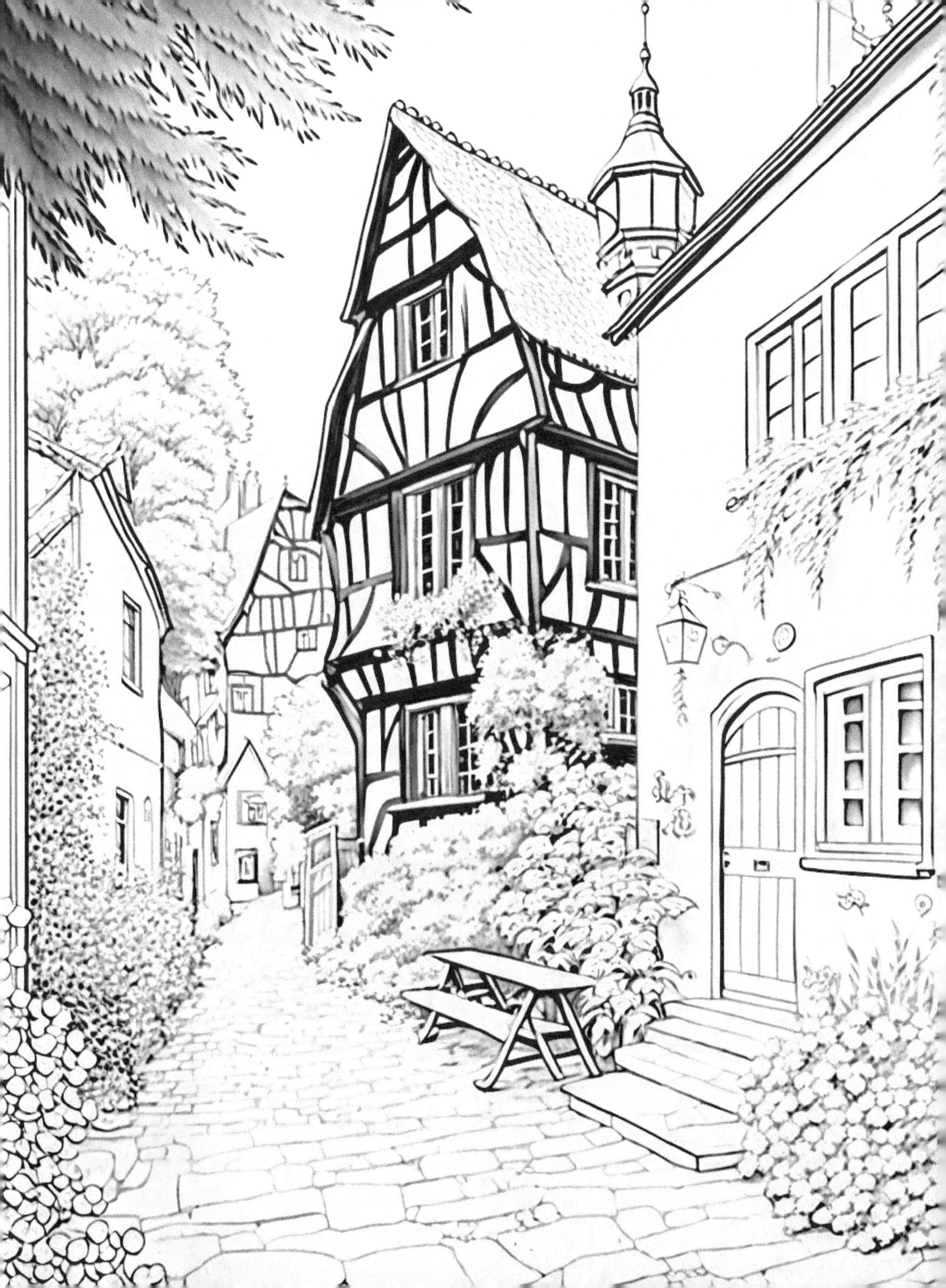

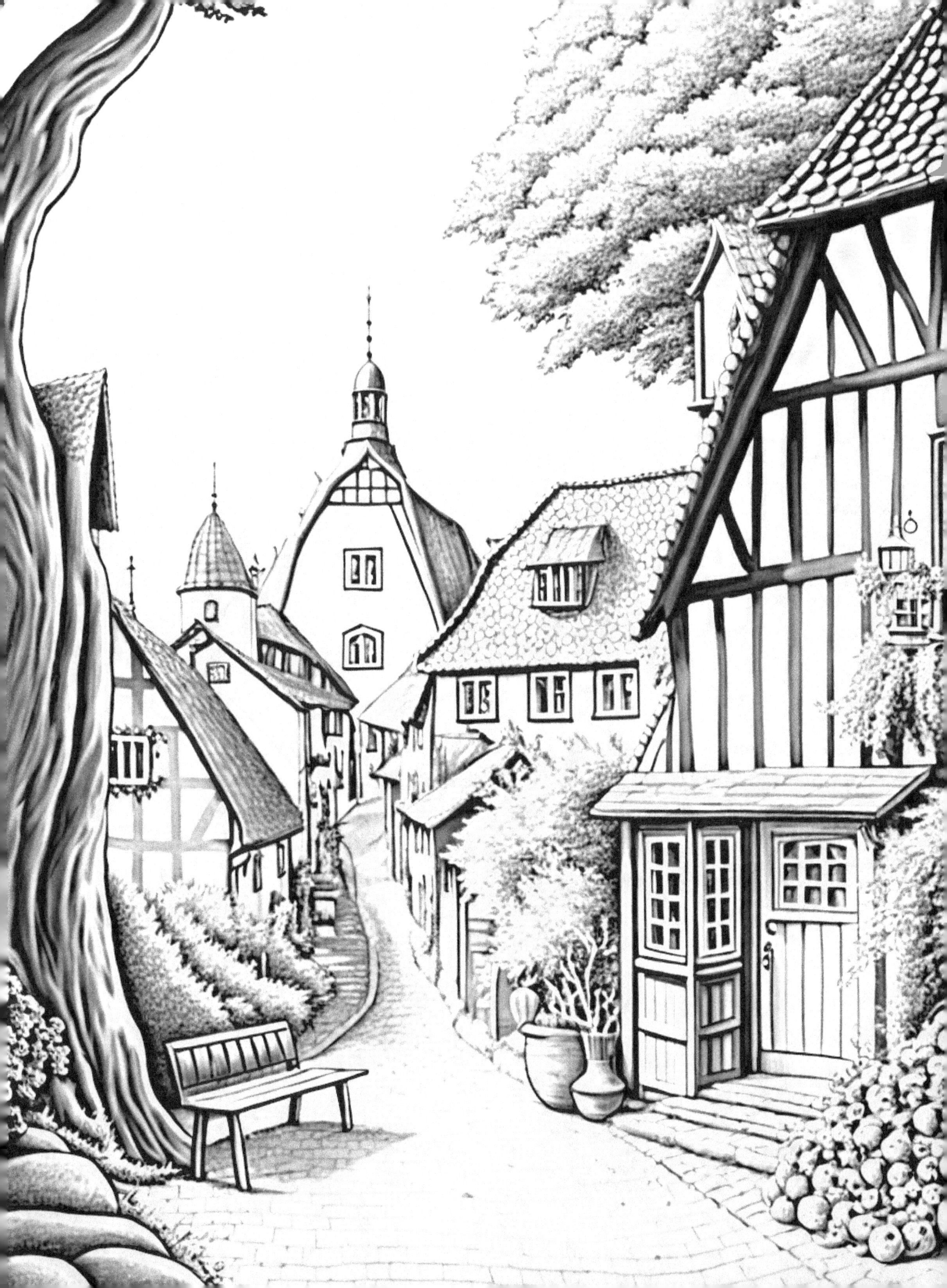

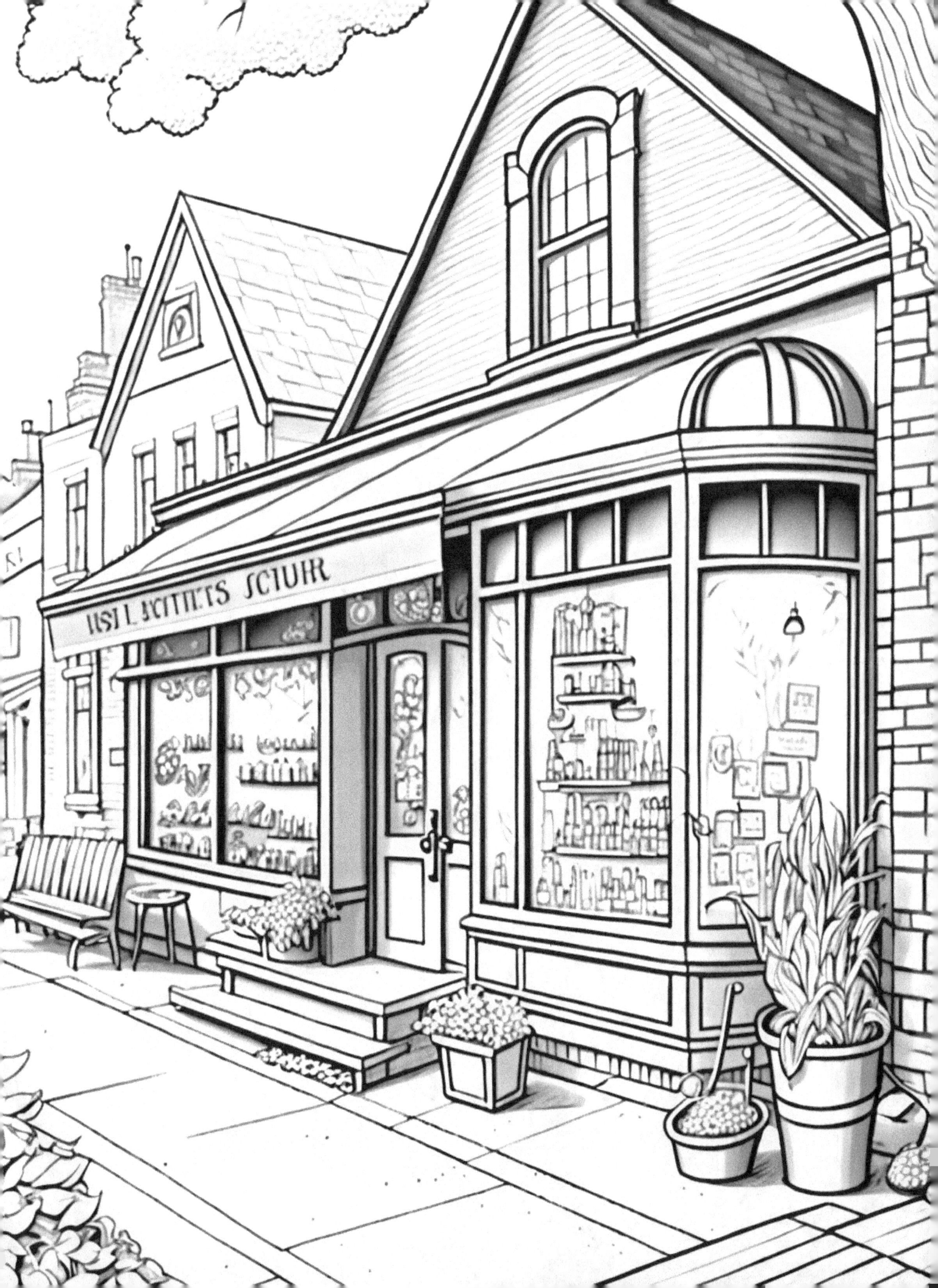

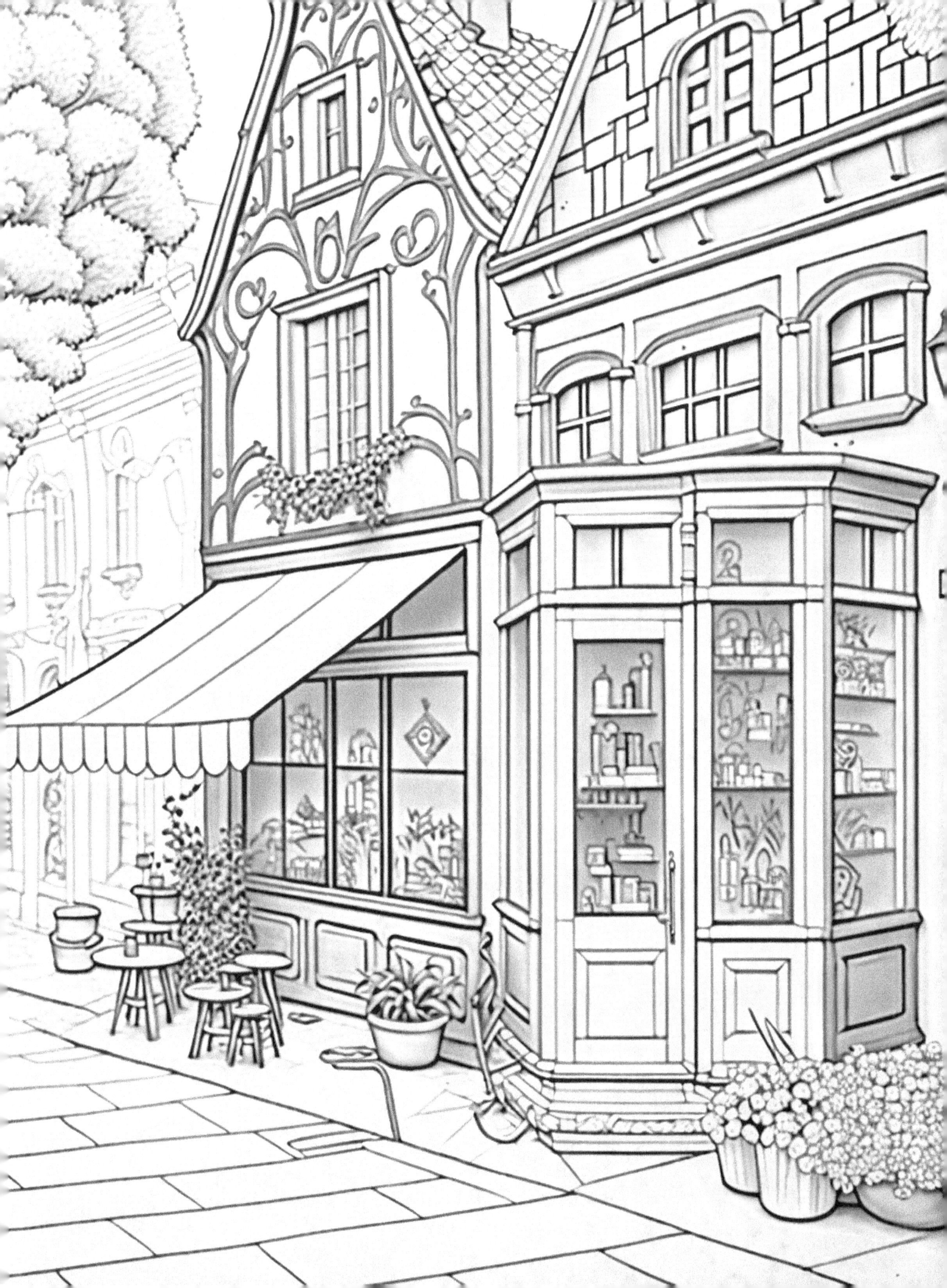

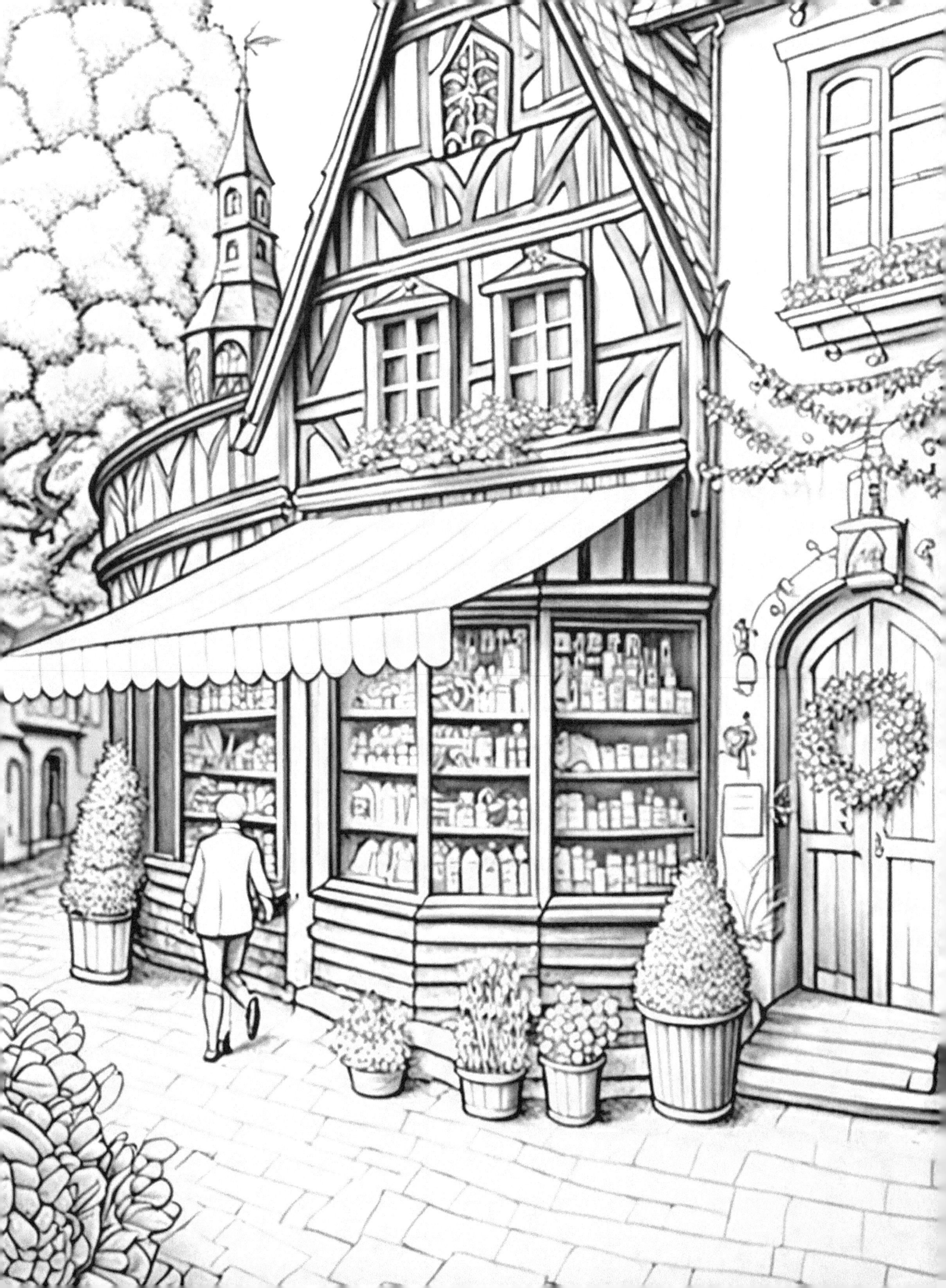

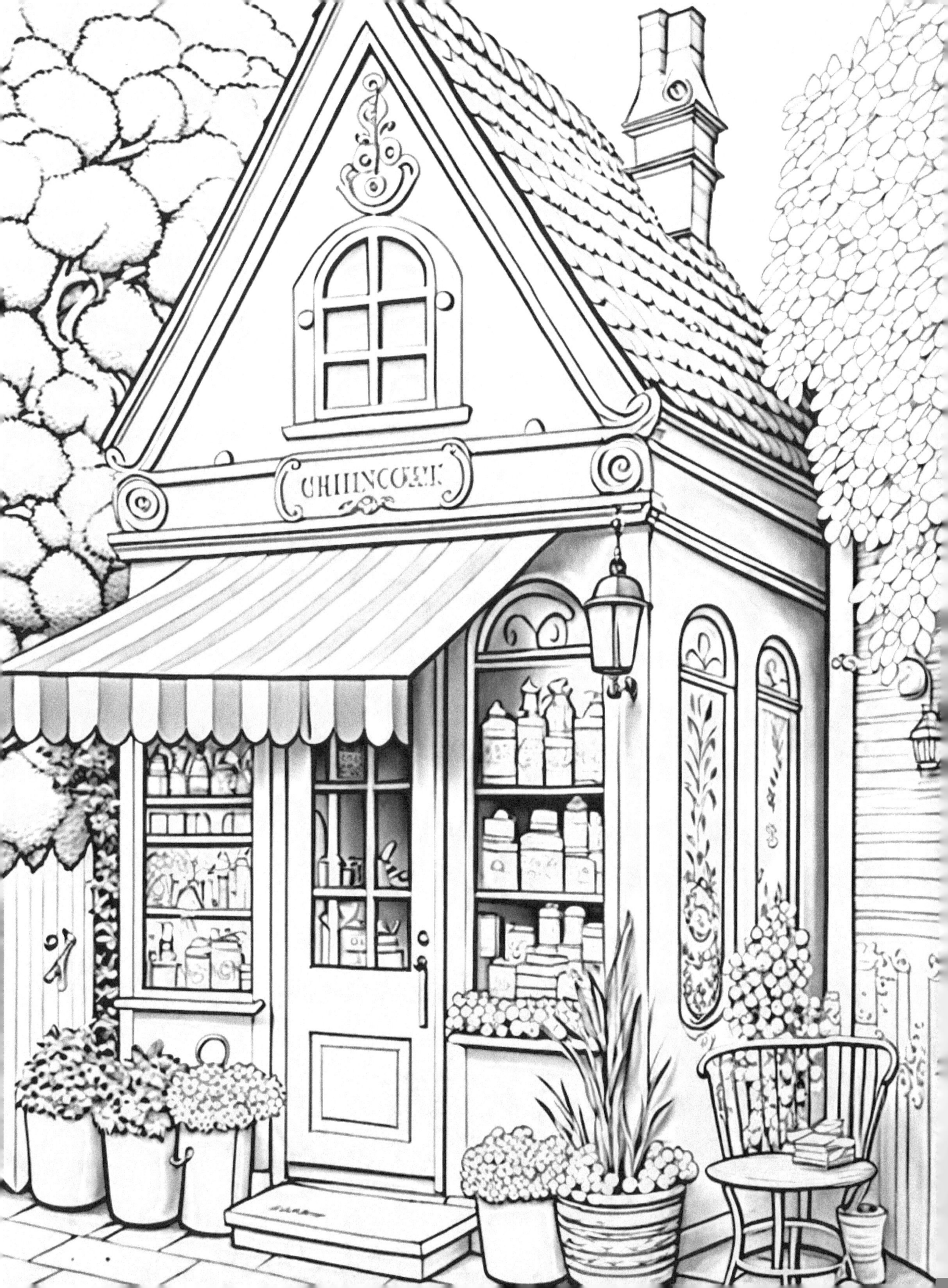

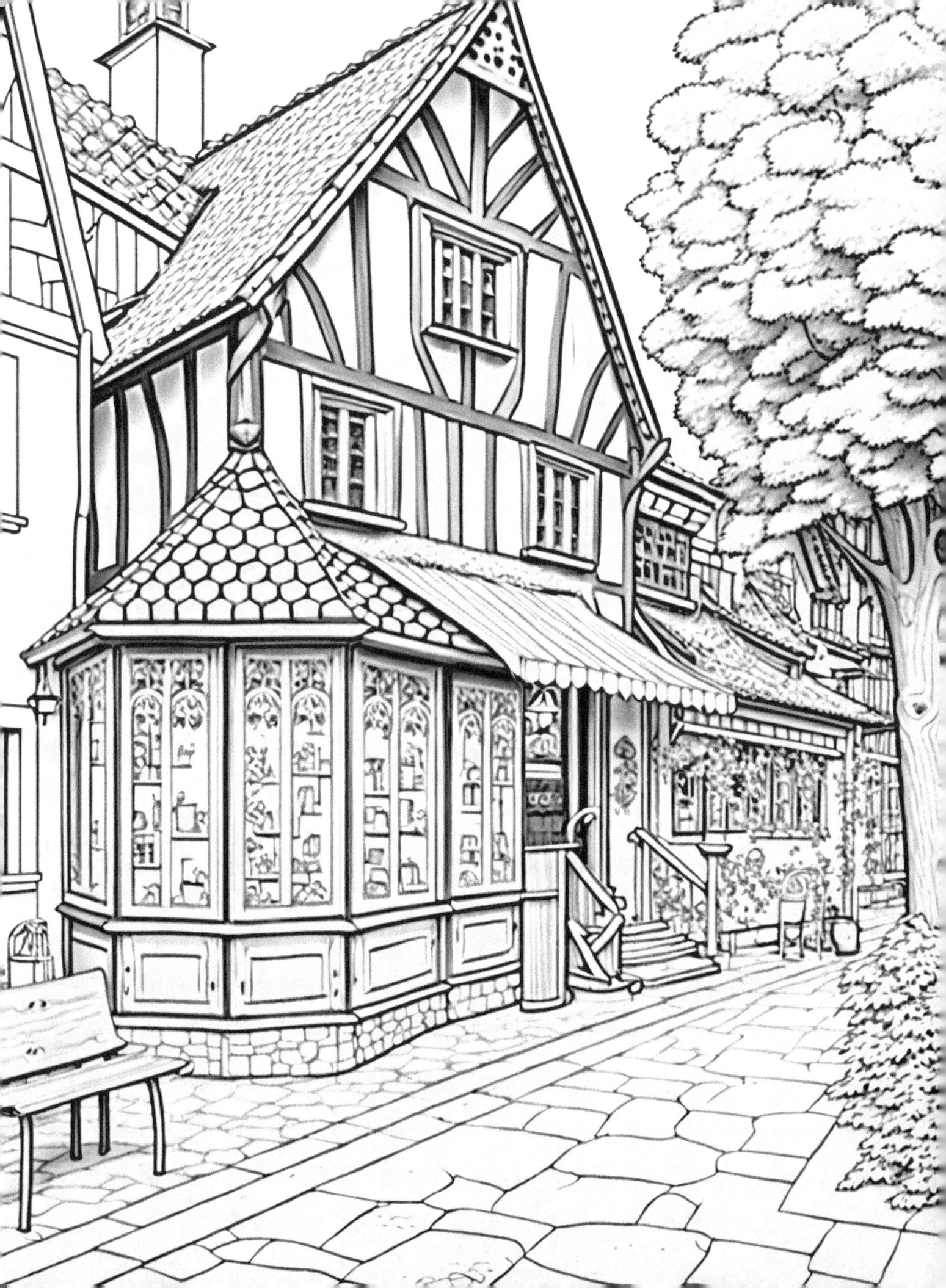

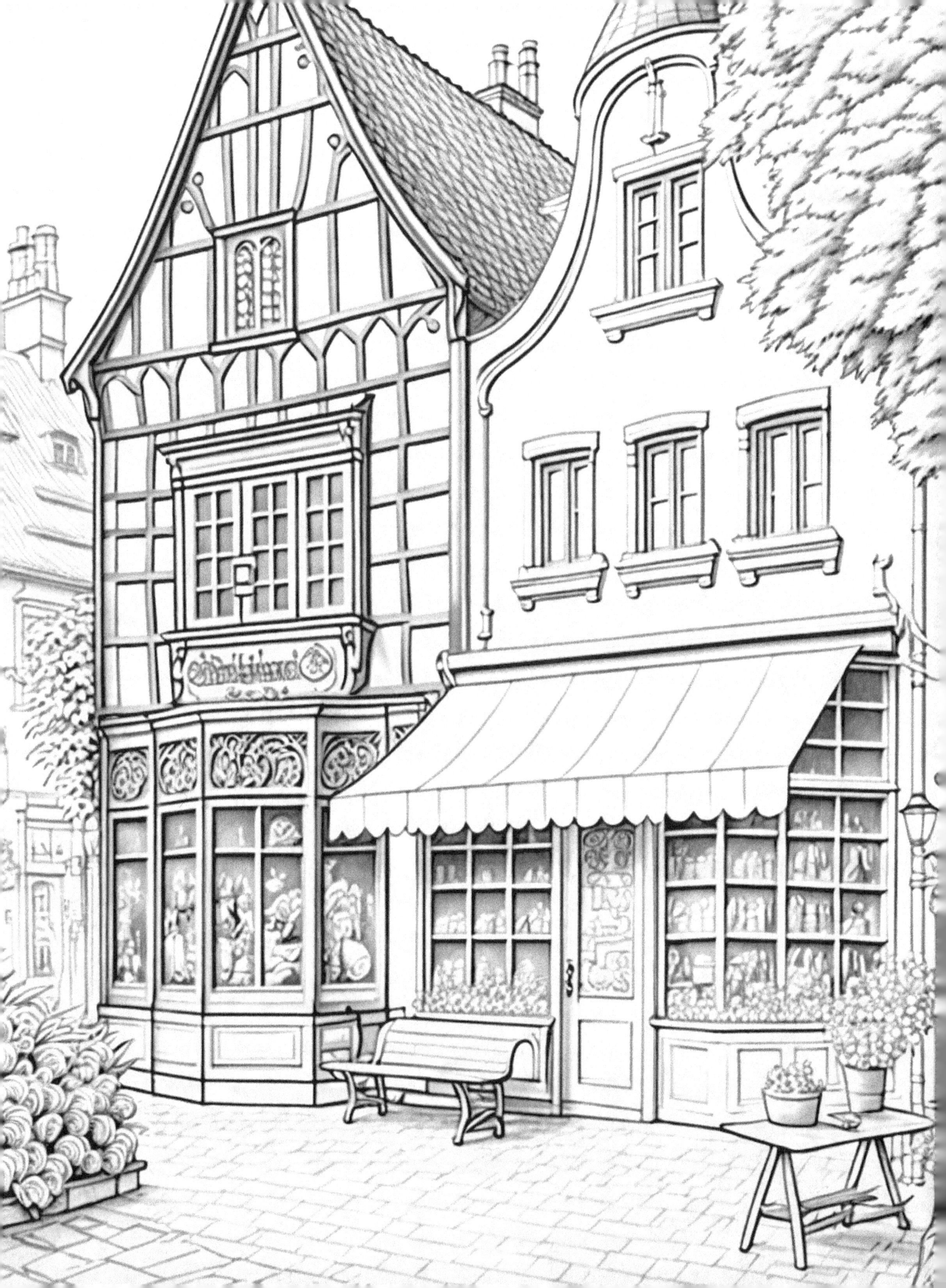

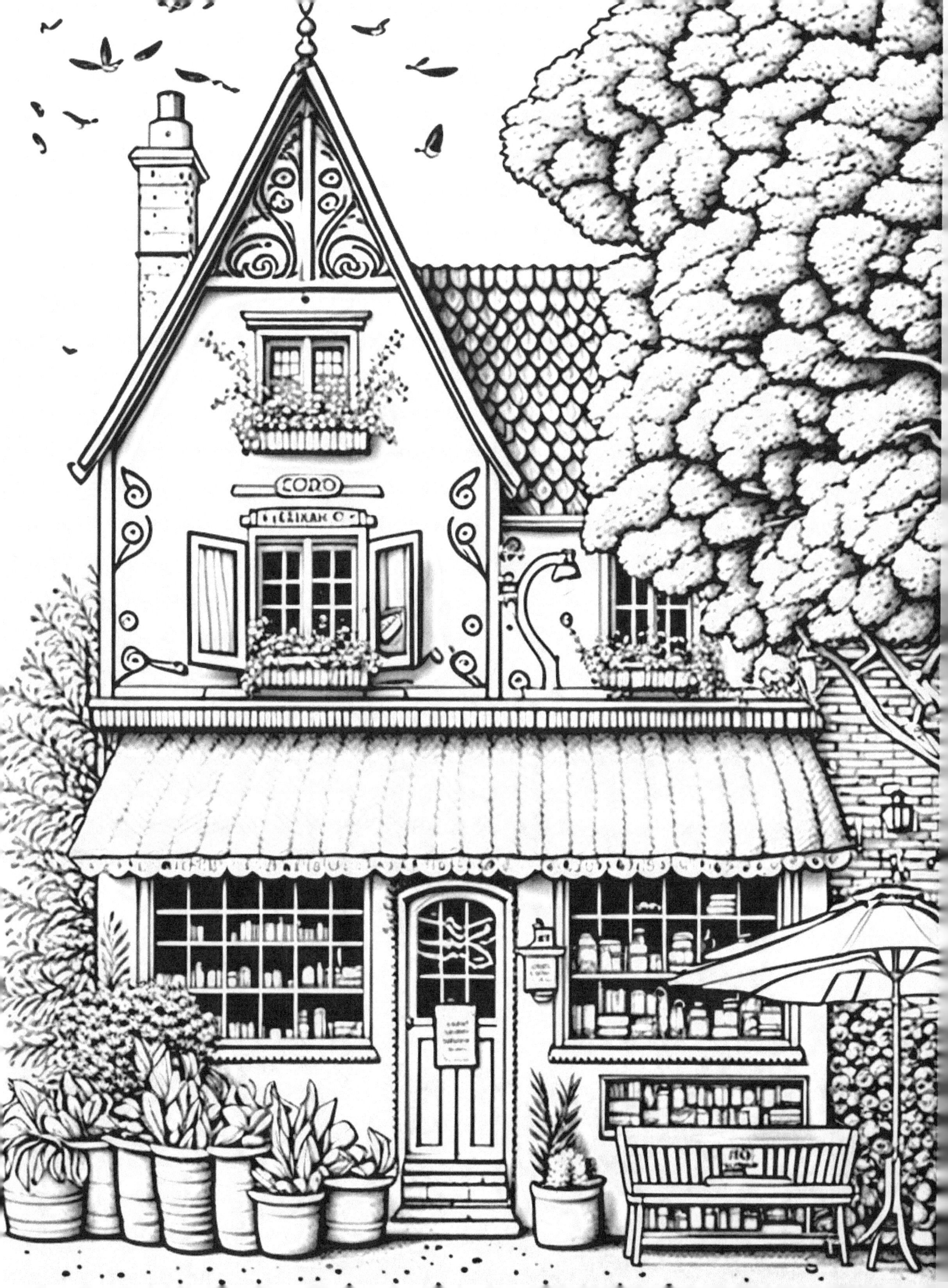

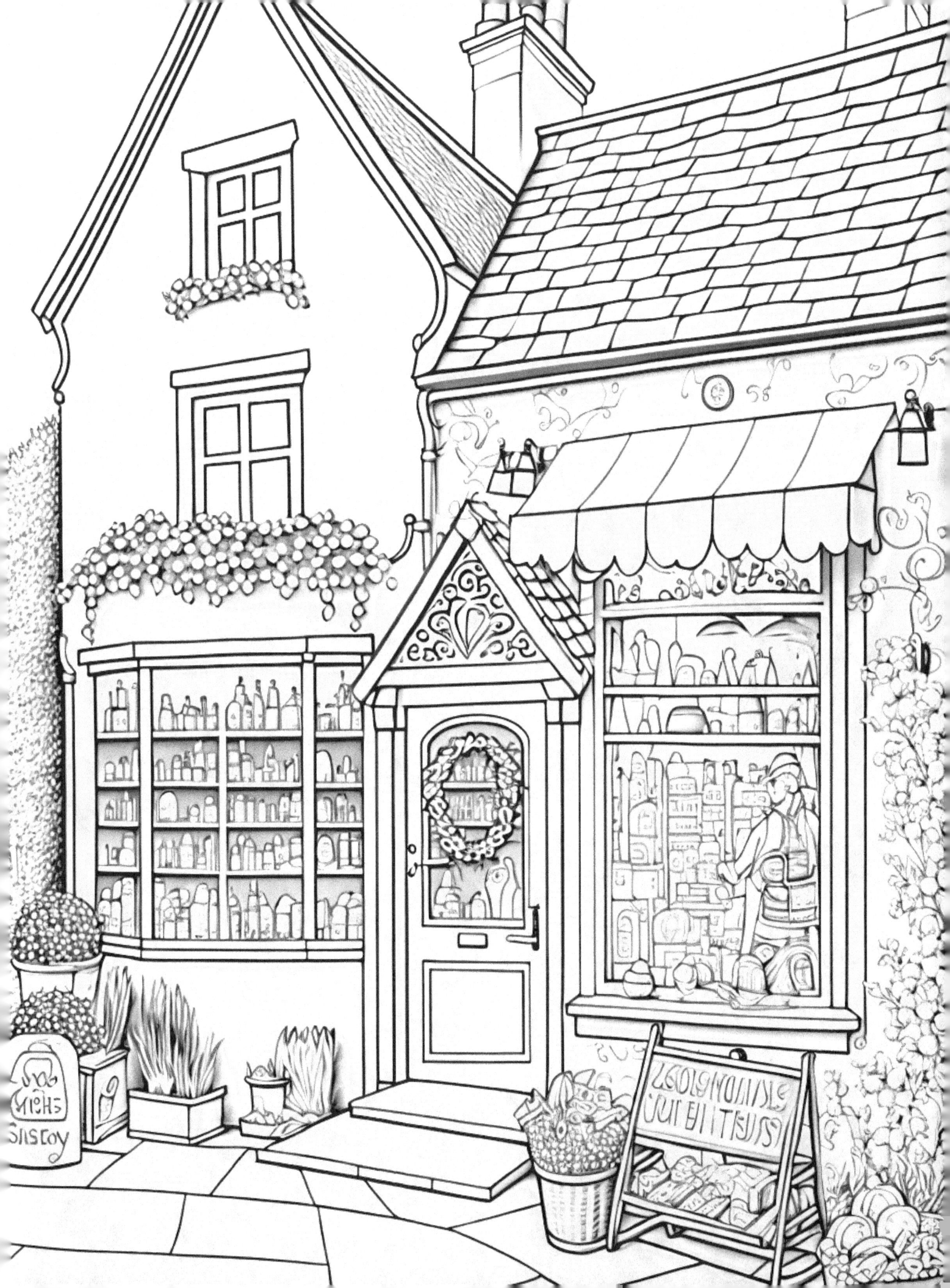

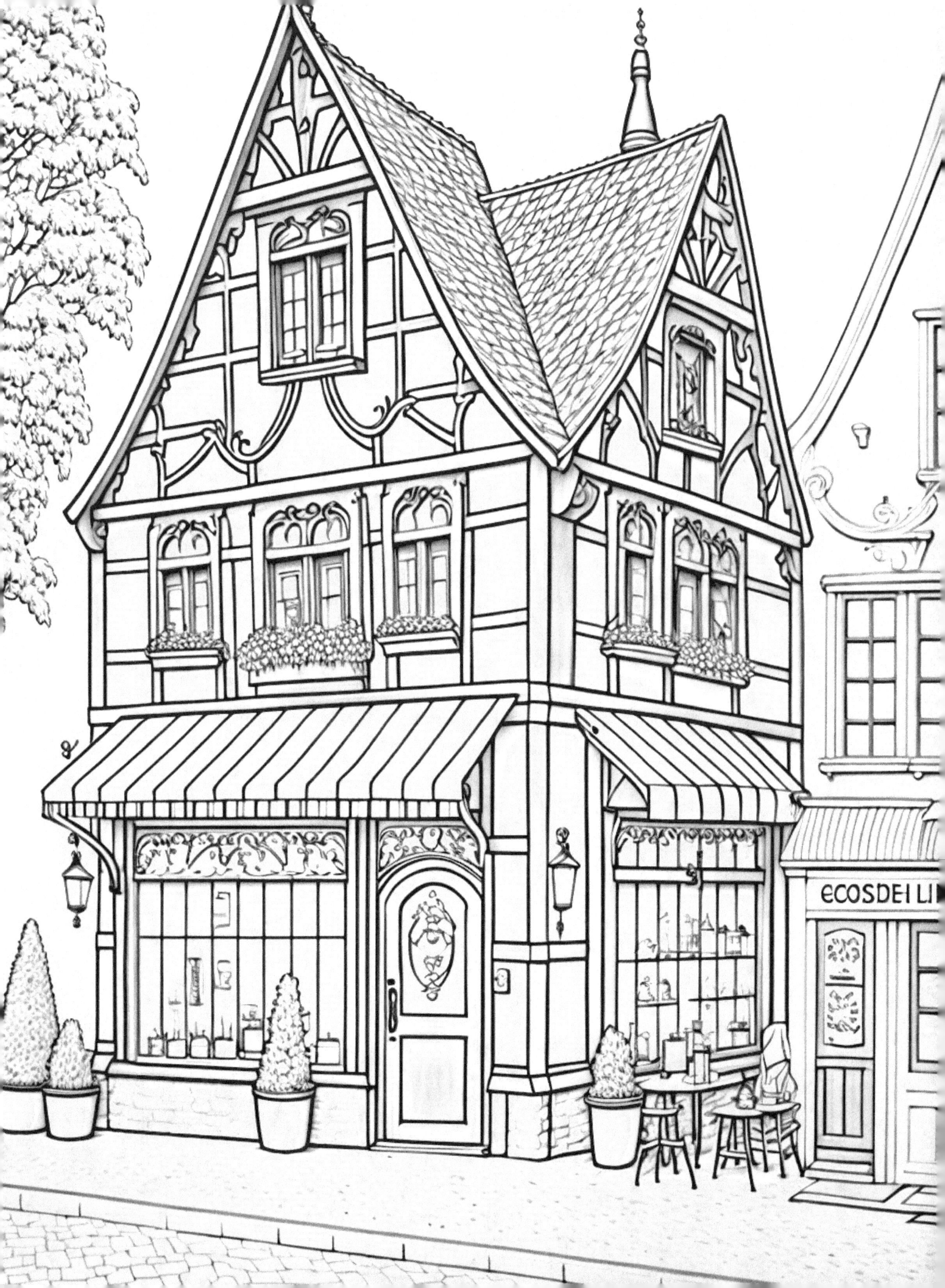

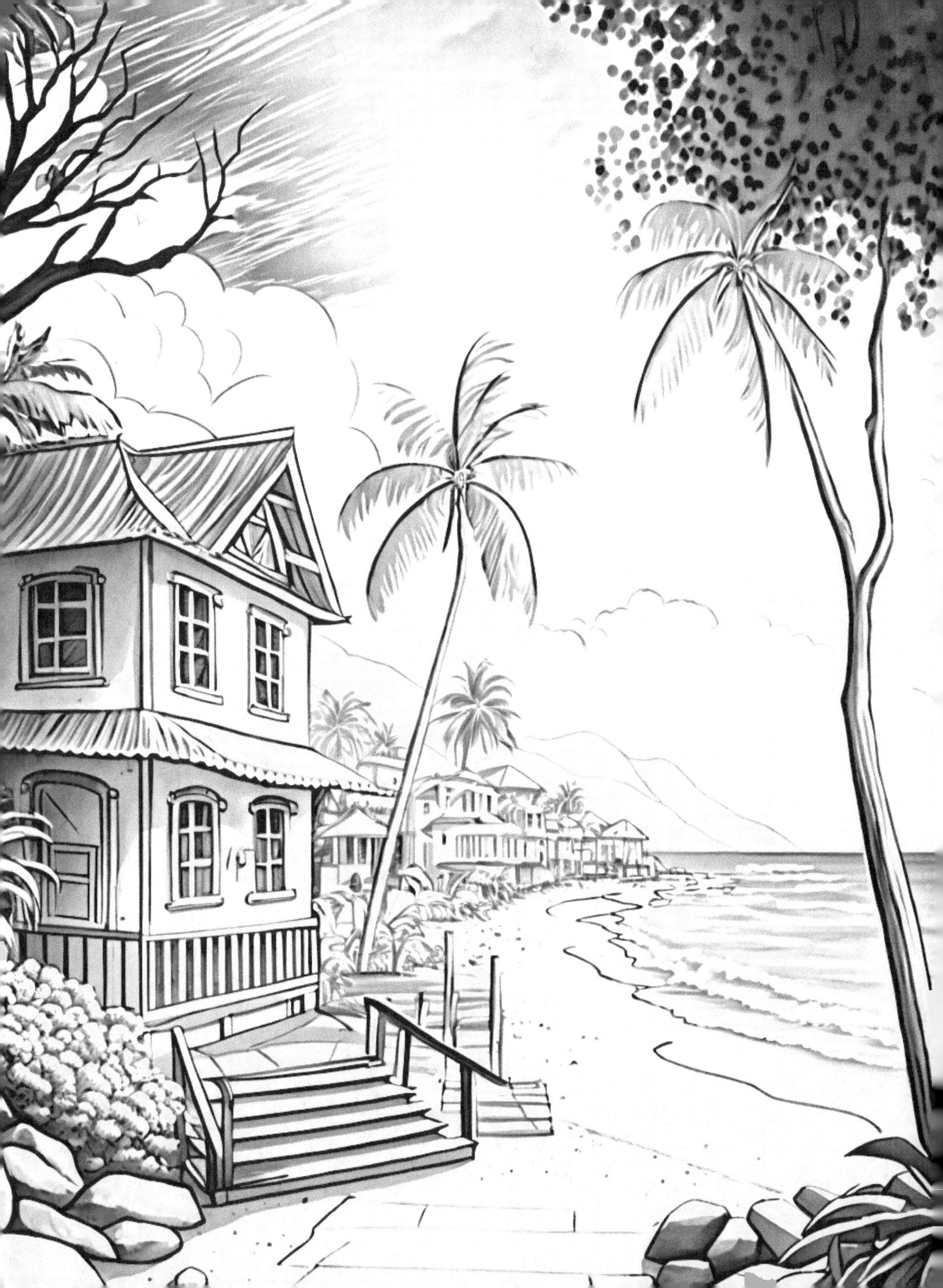

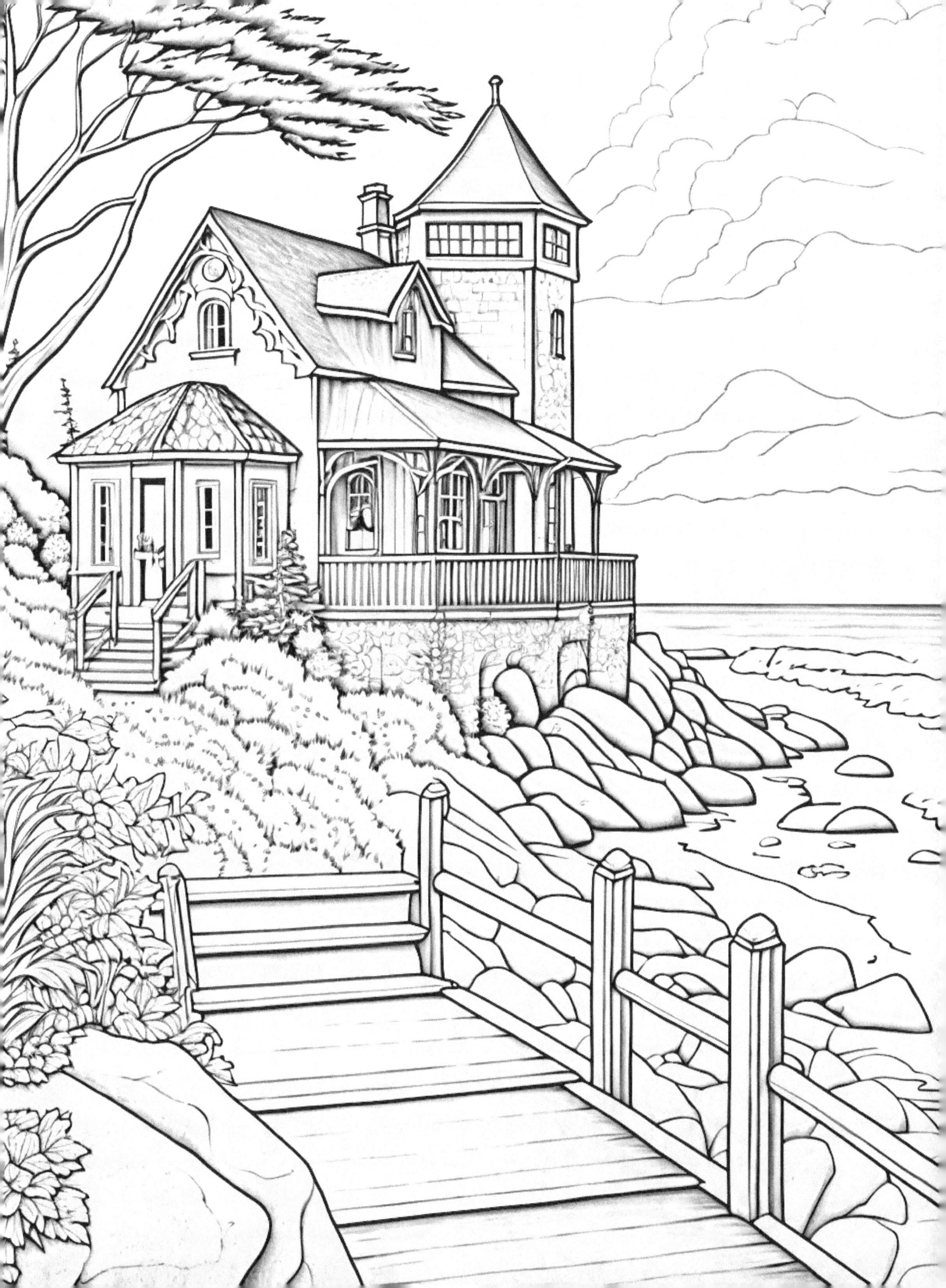

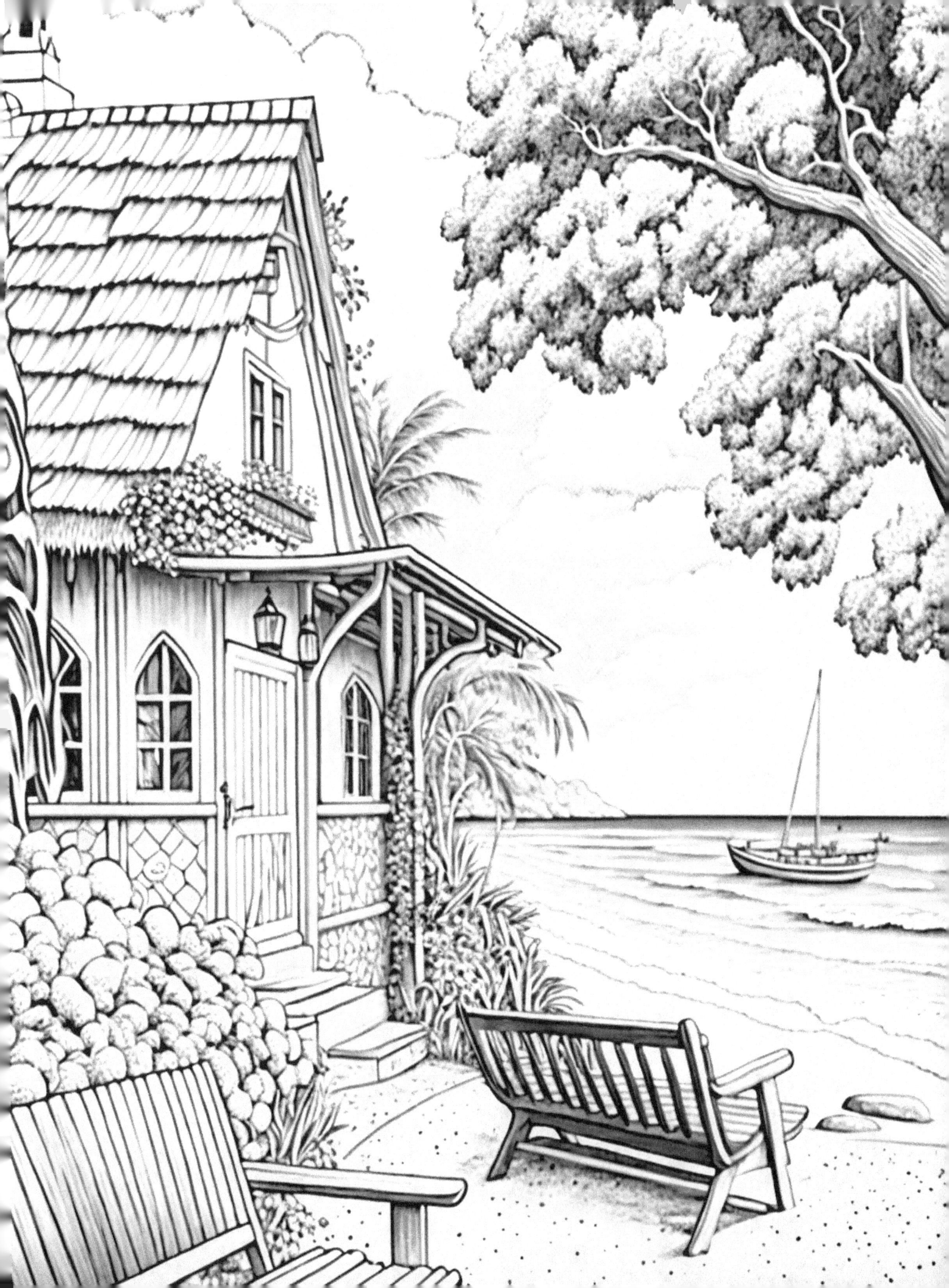

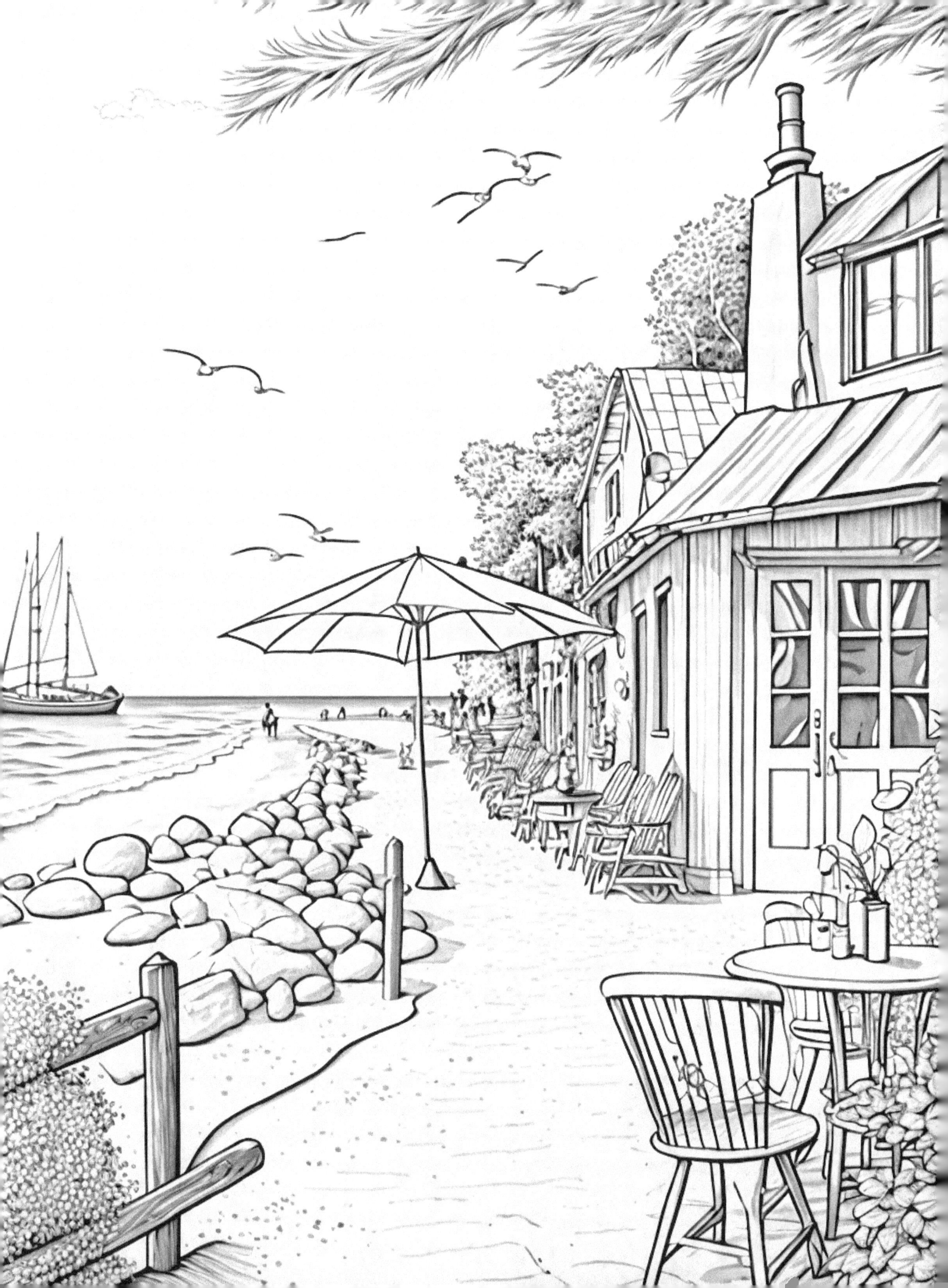

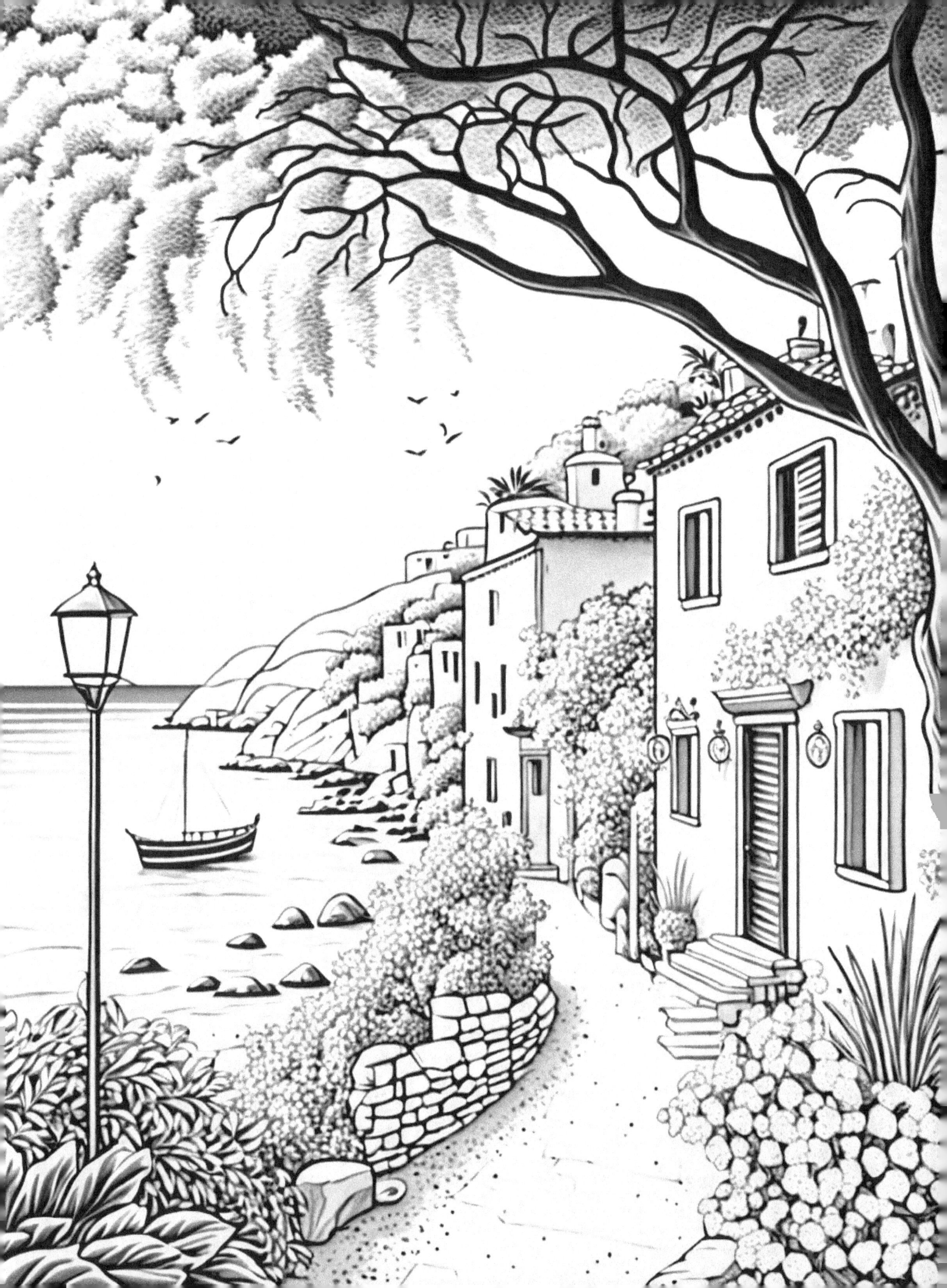

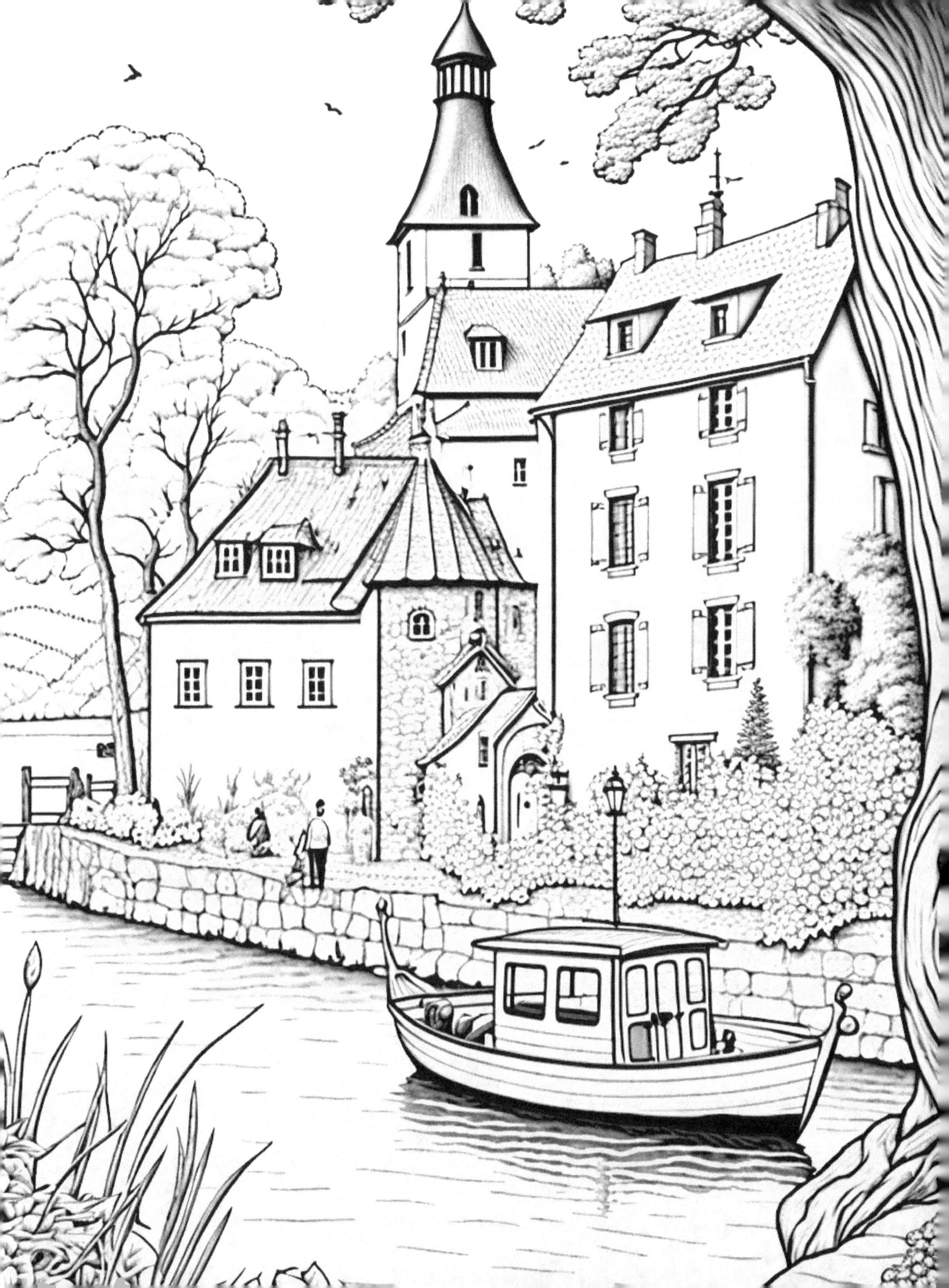

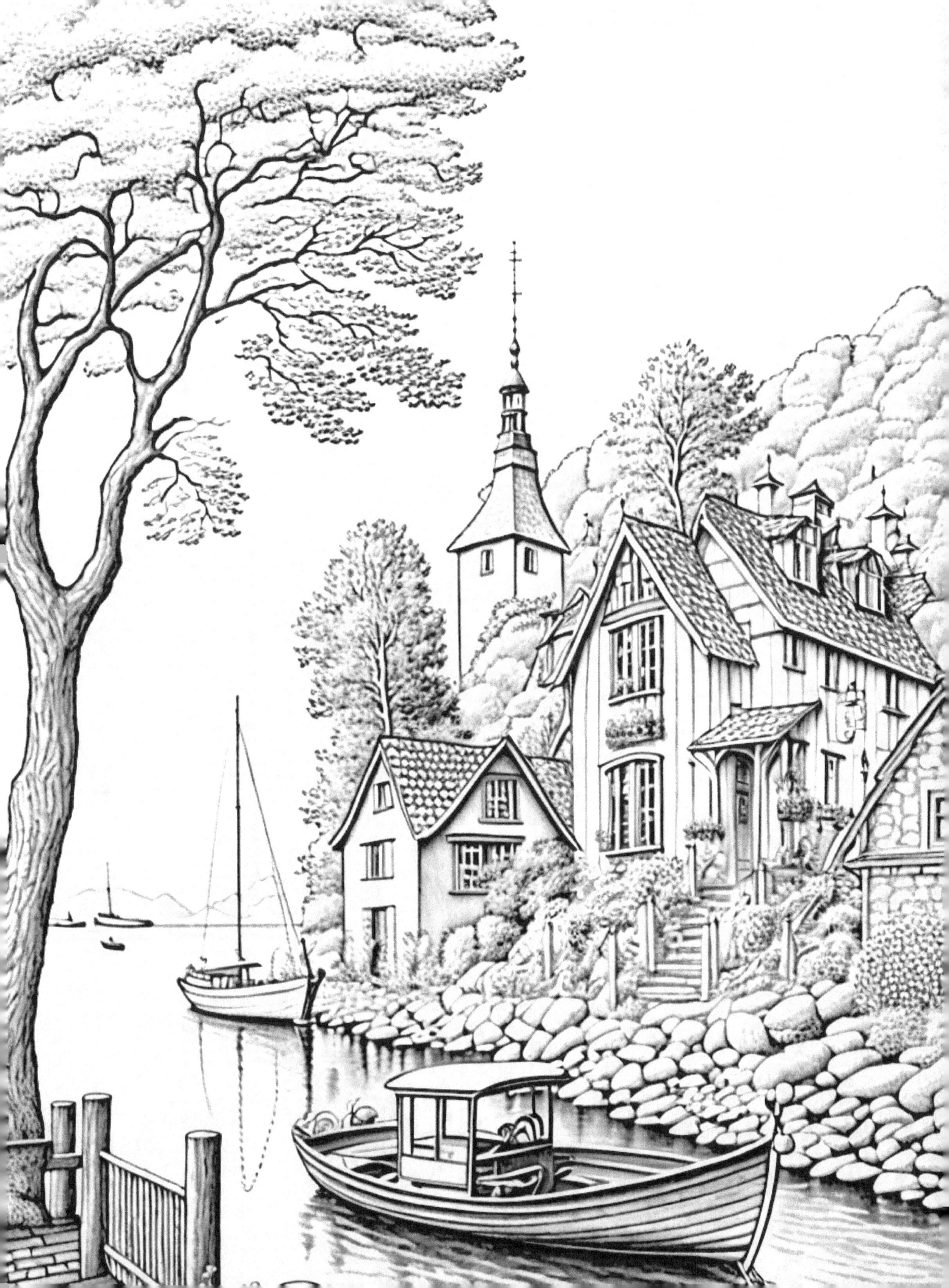

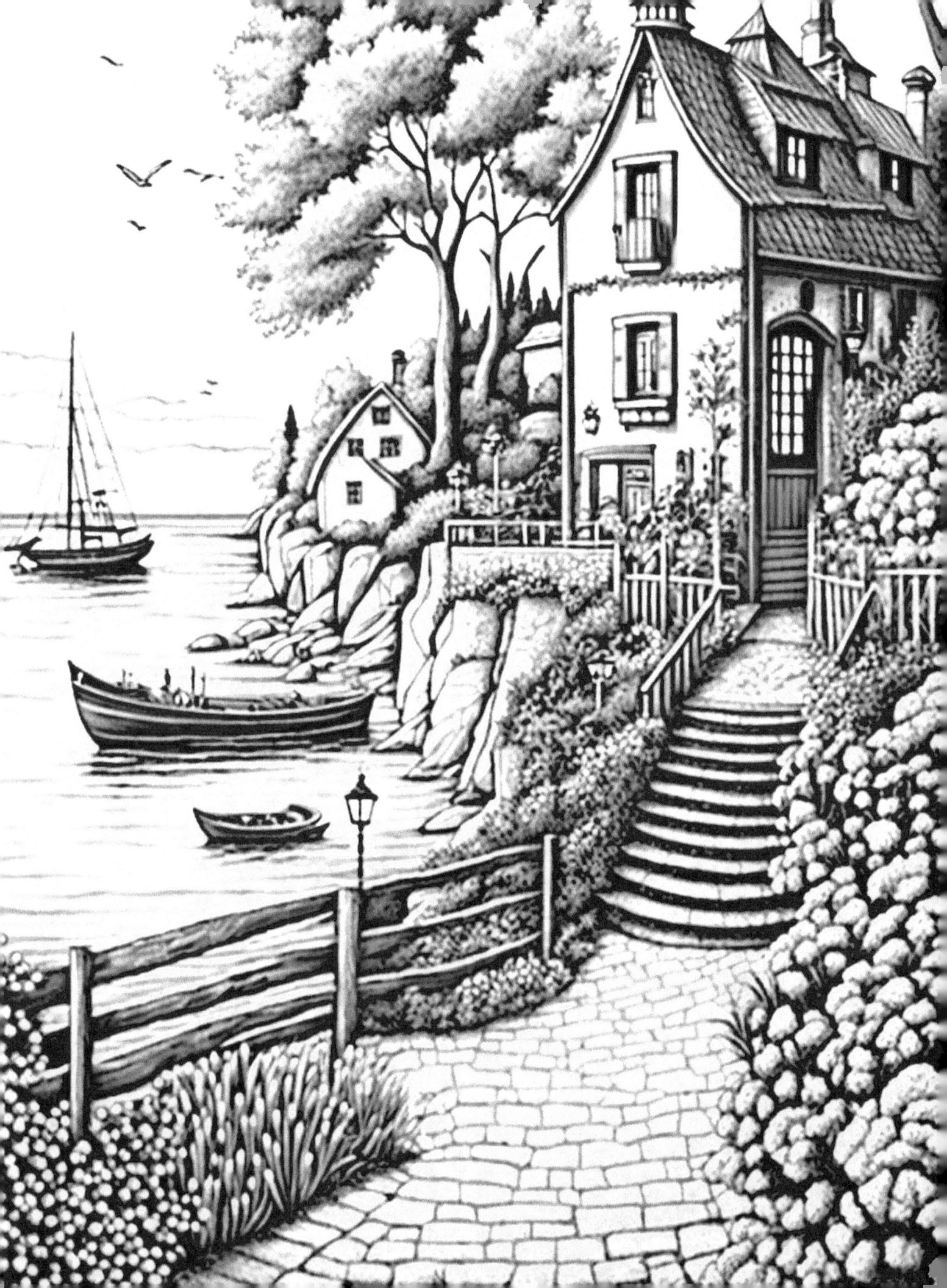

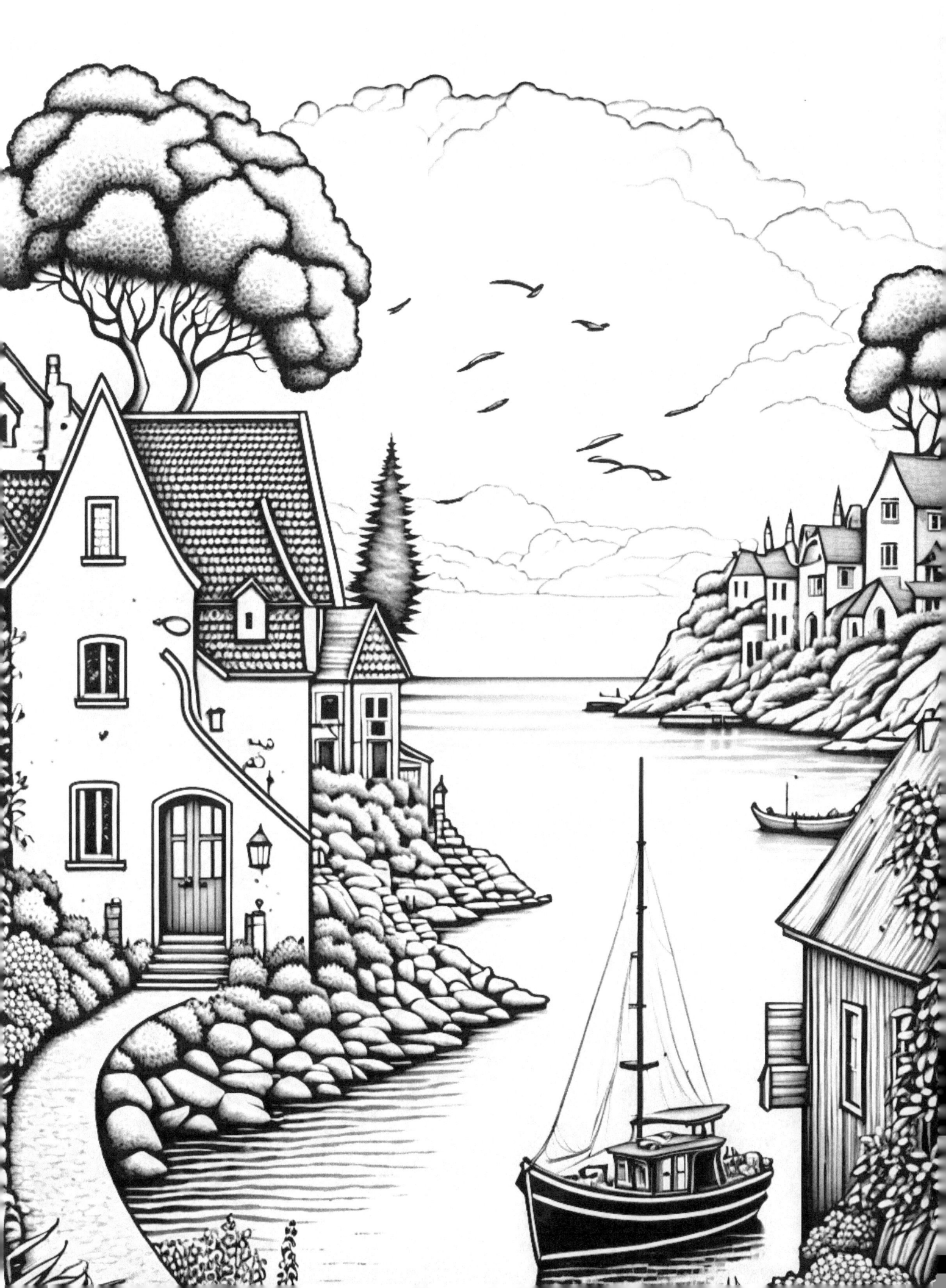

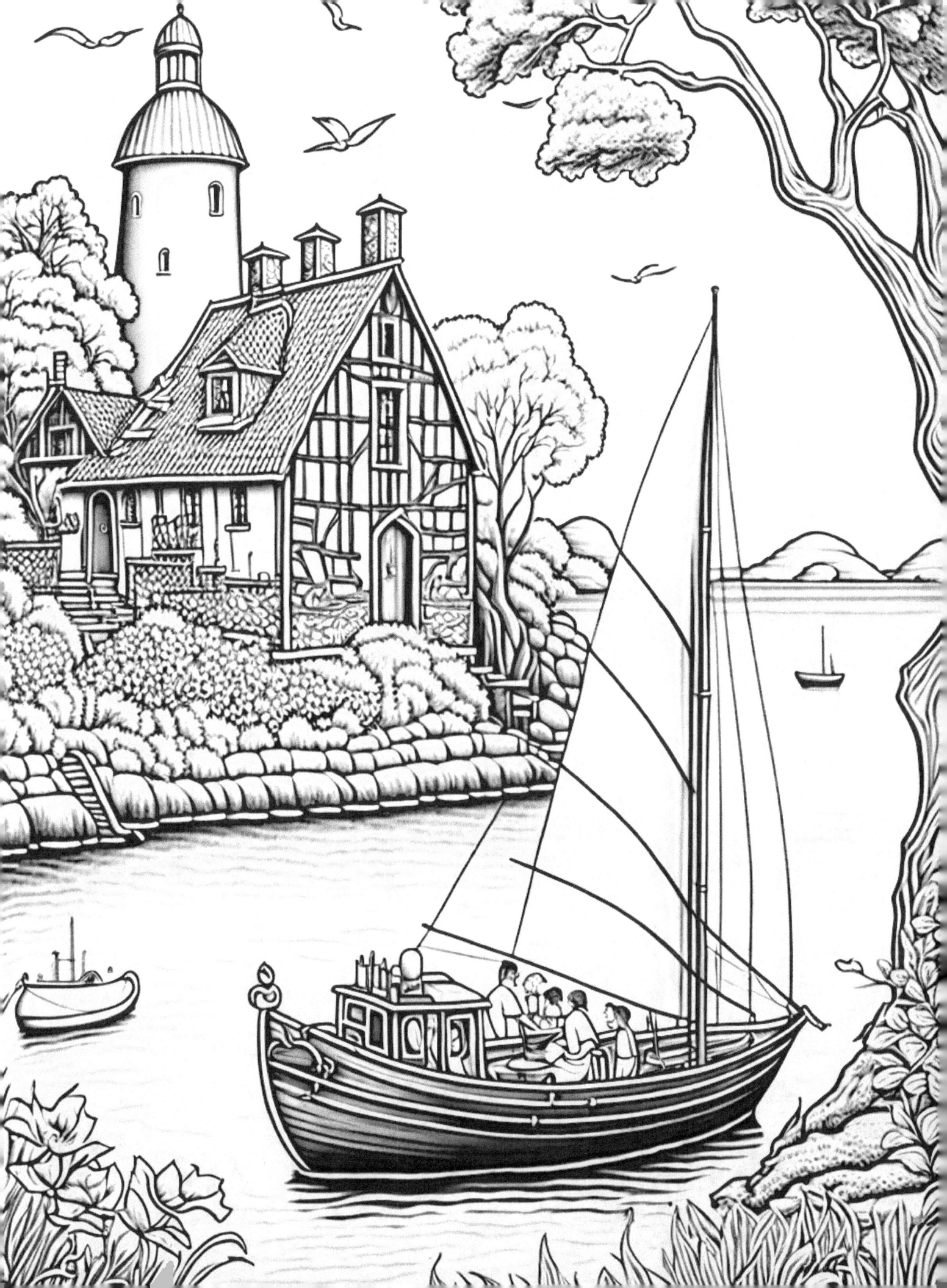

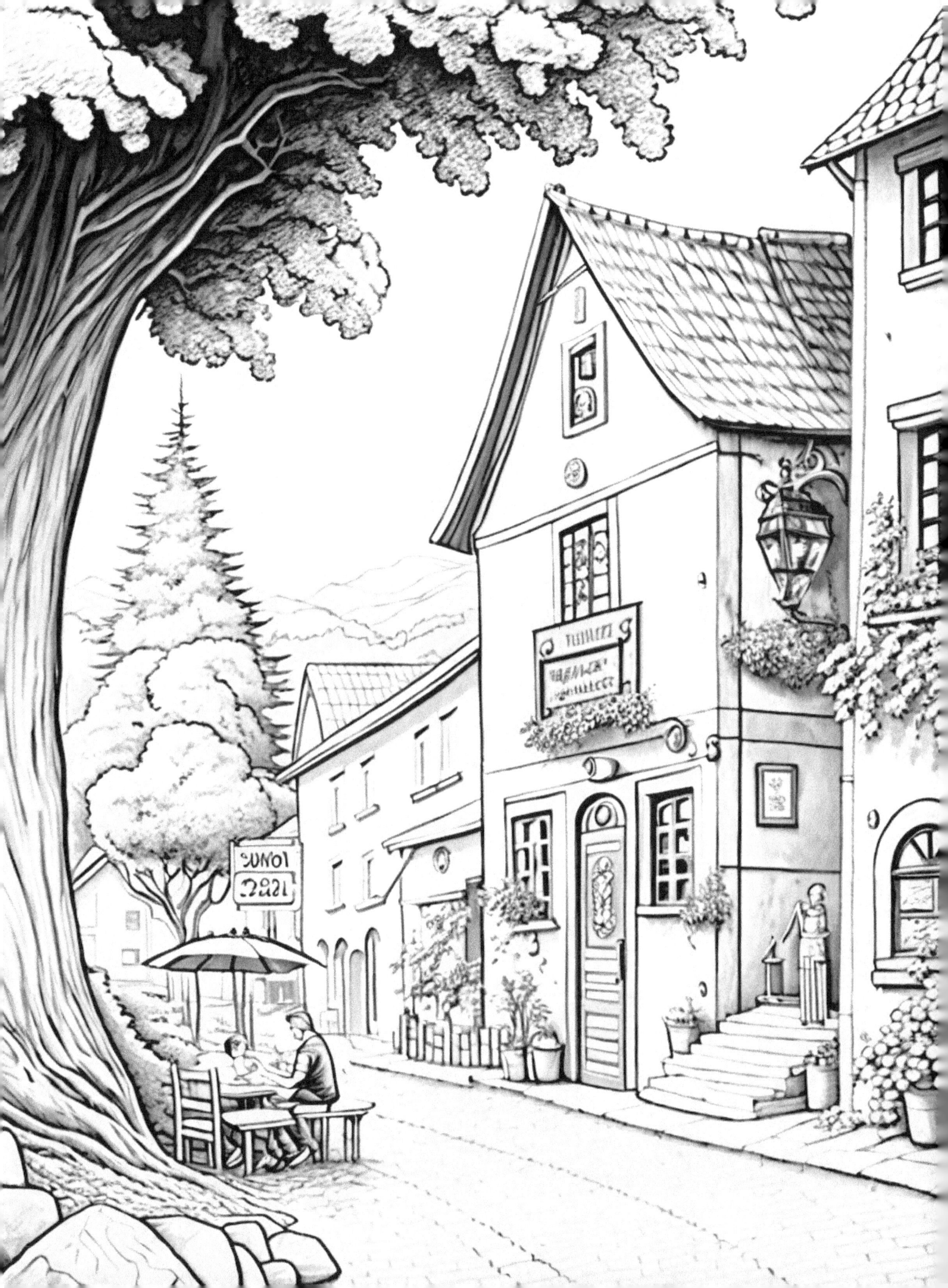

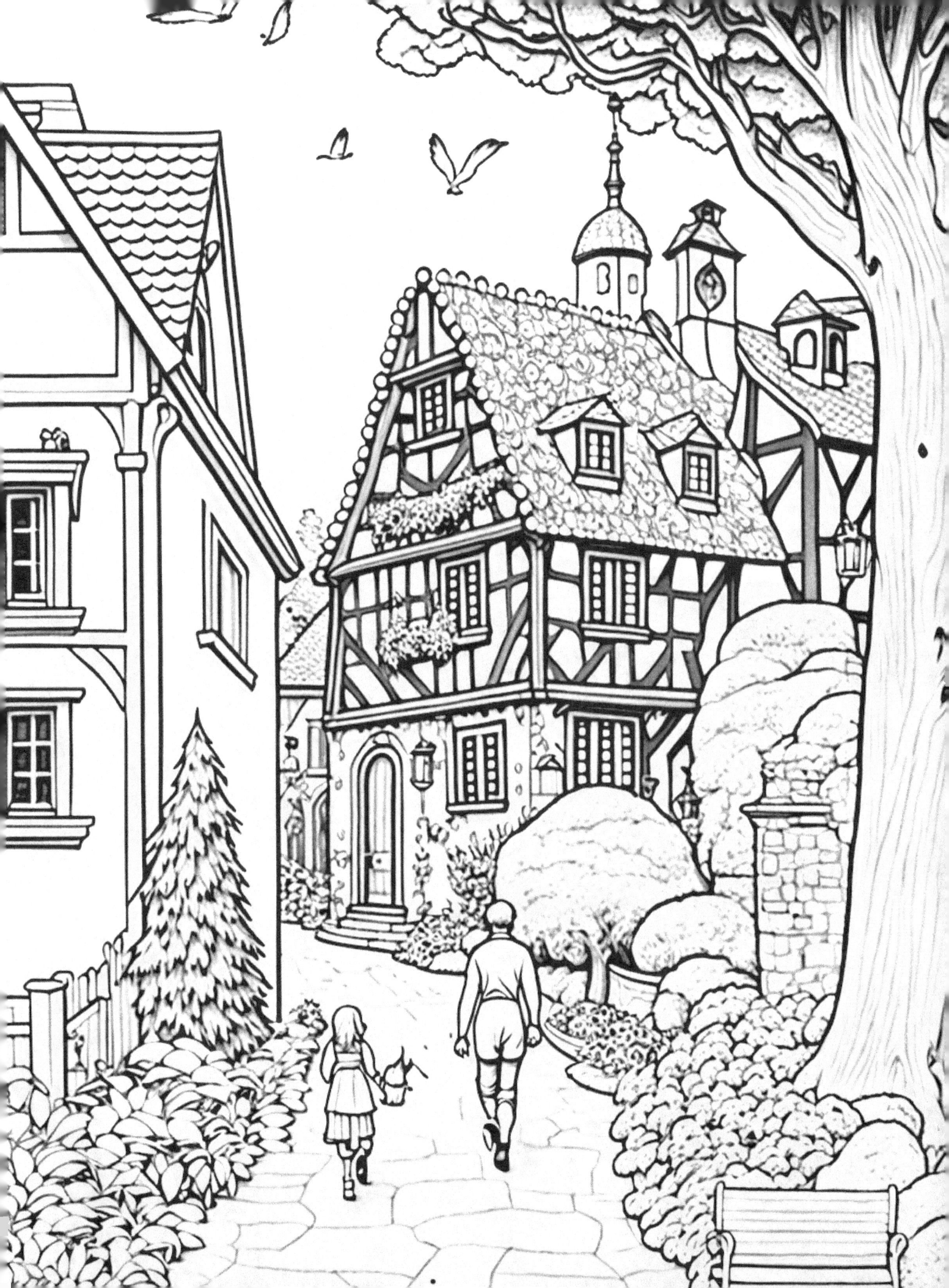

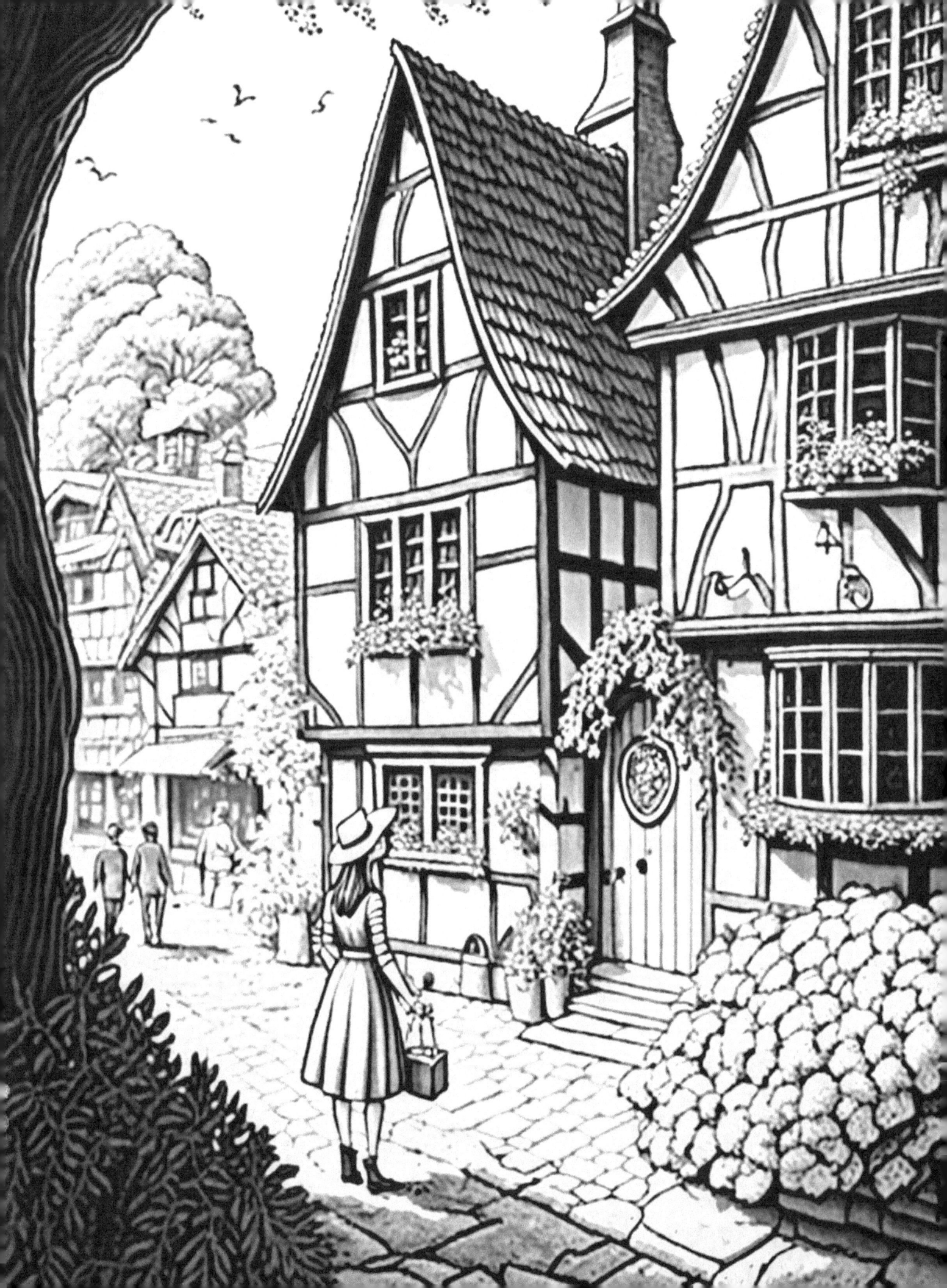

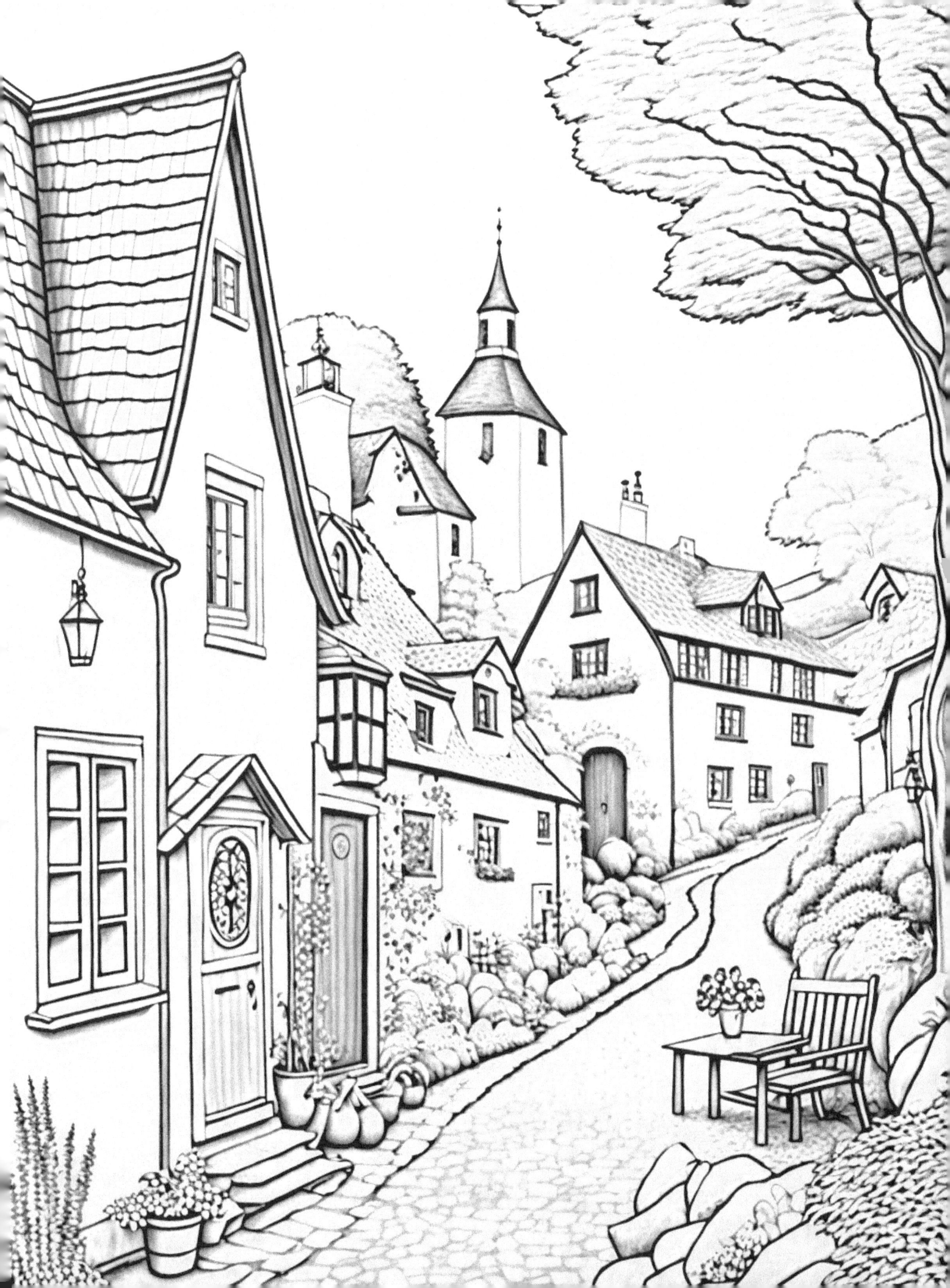

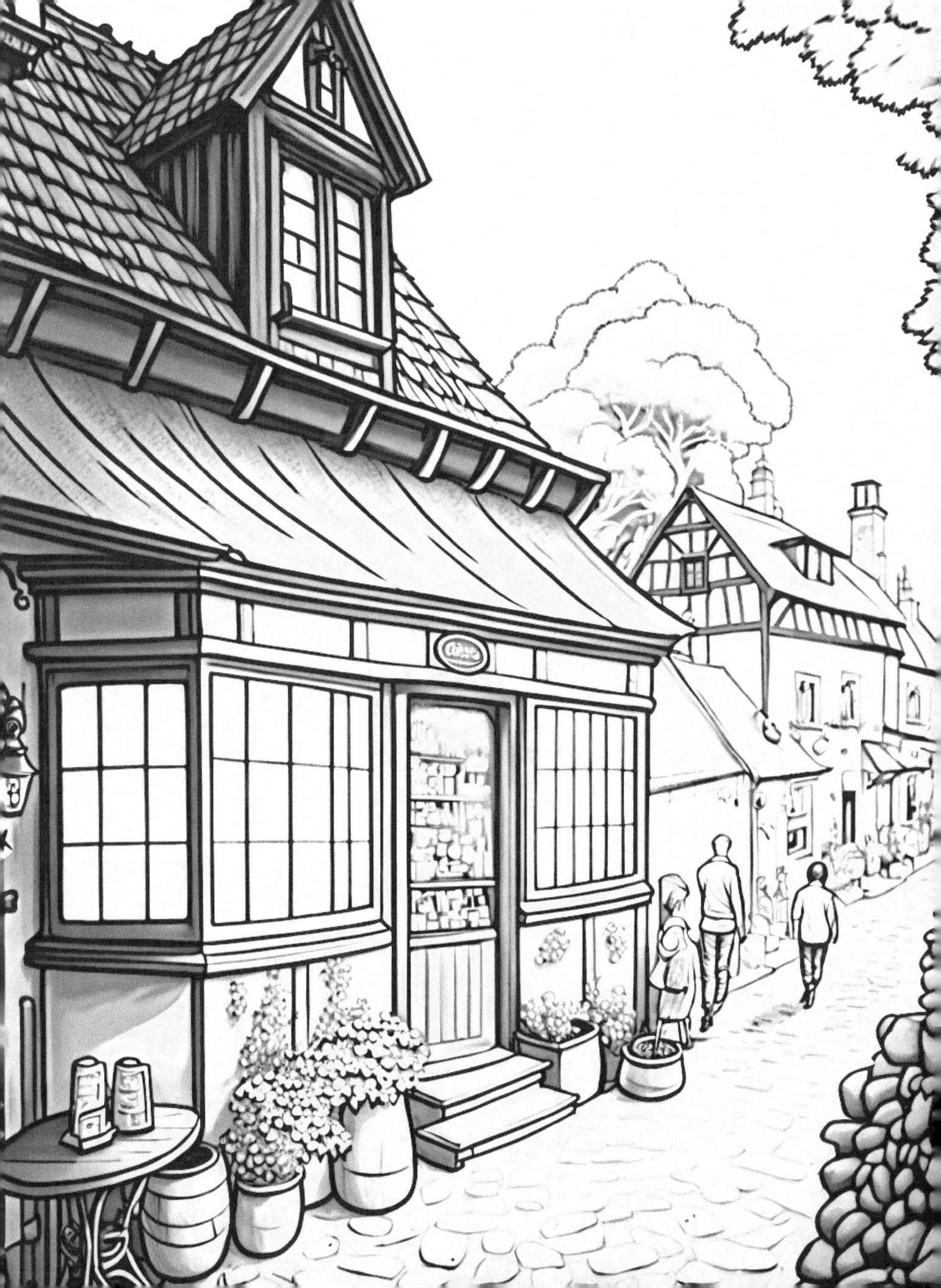

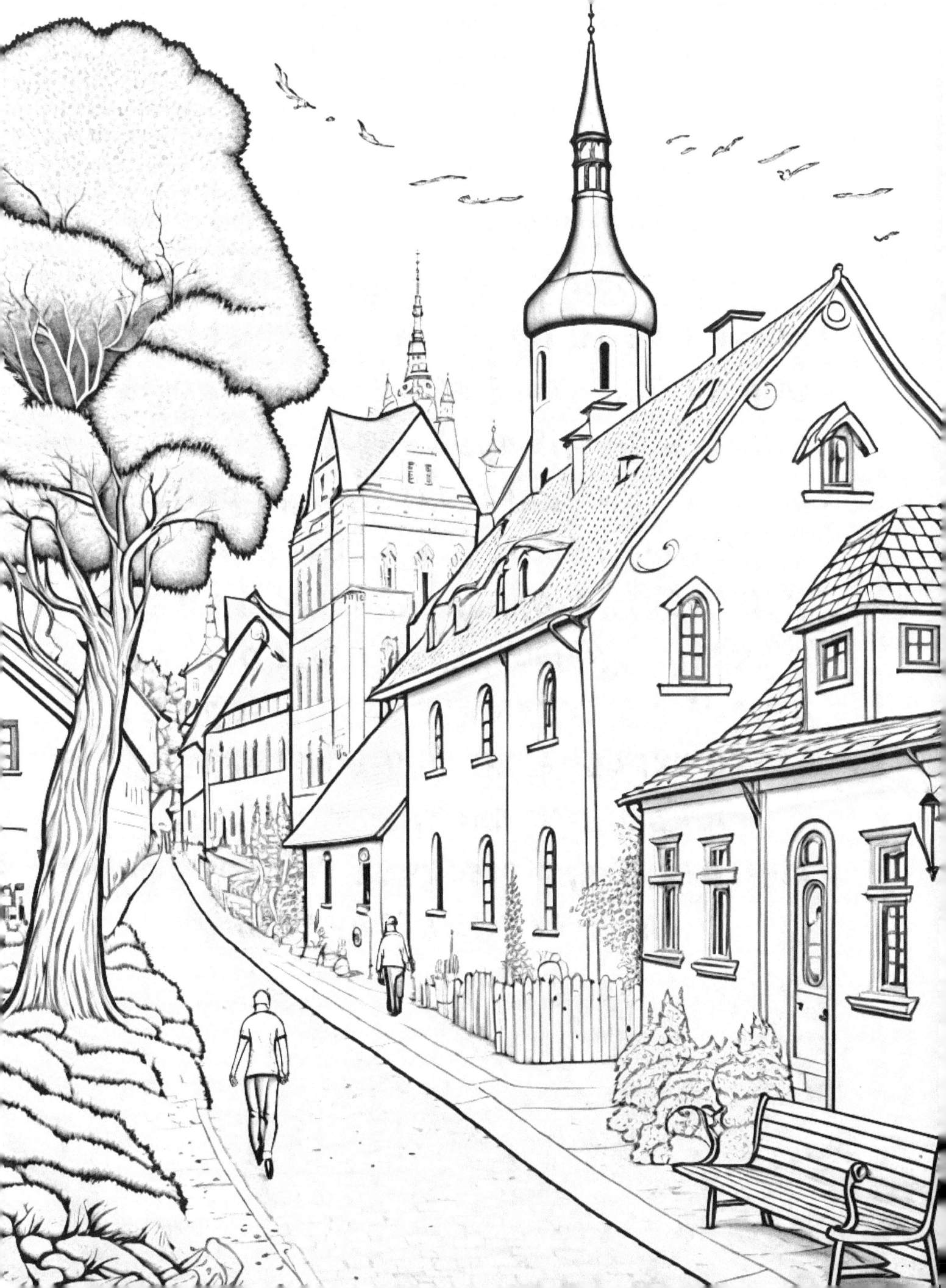

IF YOU ENJOYED OUR "COLORFUL COUNTRYSIDE" COLORING BOOK, WE WOULD LIKE TO INVITE YOU TO CHECK OUT OUR OTHER TITLES AS WELL. WE HAVE A VARIETY OF THEMES THAT ARE SURE TO CAPTURE YOUR IMAGINATION AND PROVIDE YOU WITH HOURS OF COLORING ENJOYMENT. FROM ENCHANTING GARDENS TO EXOTIC ANIMALS, EACH BOOK OFFERS A UNIQUE AND INTRICATE DESIGN FOR YOU TO EXPLORE. SO WHY NOT TREAT YOURSELF TO ANOTHER COLORING ADVENTURE AND DISCOVER THE JOYS OF CREATIVITY AND RELAXATION?

www.ingramcontent.com/pod-product-compliance
Lightning Source LLC
Chambersburg PA
CBHW081626220526
45467CB00029B/3059